Everybody Wins!

Non-Competitive Party Games & Activities for Children

Jody L. Blosser

Foreword by Gaylyn Larned, Ph.D.

Illustrated by Richard Salvucci

Sterling Publishing Co., Inc. New York

Dedication

This book is dedicated to my children, Kelly, Glen, and William.

Acknowledgment

I would like to thank my mother, Carole Dickey, for all the help and encouragement she gave me while I was working on this book.

Library of Congress Cataloging-in-Publication Data

Blosser, Jody L.
    Everybody wins! : non-competitive party games & activities for children / Jody L. Blosser ; foreword and charts by Gaylyn Larned ; illustrated by Richard Salvucci.
        p.   cm.
    Includes index.
    ISBN 0-8069-6102-3
    1. Games. 2. Children's parties. 3. Cooperativeness in children.
I. Title.
GV1203.B613   1996
793'.01922—dc20   95-39394
                                                                CIP

10 9 8 7 6 5 4 3 2 1

Published by Sterling Publishing Company, Inc.
387 Park Avenue South, New York, N.Y. 10016
© 1996 by Jody L. Blosser
Foreword and charts © 1996 by Gaylyn Larned, Ph.D.
Distributed in Canada by Sterling Publishing
% Canadian Manda Group, One Atlantic Avenue, Suite 105
Toronto, Ontario, Canada M6K 3E7
Distributed in Great Britain and Europe by Cassell PLC
Wellington House, 125 Strand, London WC2R 0BB, England
Distributed in Australia by Capricorn Link (Australia) Pty Ltd.
P.O. Box 6651, Baulkham Hills, Business Centre, NSW 2153, Australia
Manufactured in the United States of America
All rights reserved

Sterling ISBN 0-8069-6102-3

CONTENTS

FOREWORD

I saw a stencilled pillow recently that captured the wonderful intention on every page of this delightful book. The pillow said WHO CARES *WINS*. What a pleasure to read Ms. Blosser's imaginative book of noncompetitive games and activities for children! Her approach to fun with kids will most assuredly hit the mark for all who are seeking more ways to develop well-adjusted youngsters. Probably the most important task in childhood is the identification of ourselves as people who can approach life with a certain amount of dynamism and confidence, and with a positive outlook. It's called self-esteem. And everybody wants it.

The need for self-esteem began to draw attention in our Western culture at the turn of the last century. Popularized early on in women's magazines, it was later taken up by educators and religious leaders. Today, high self-esteem is on most parents' minds, and they all want their children to have it. But how does a child develop self-esteem? The search for an answer to this question has become a treasure hunt that has occupied the time and talents of thousands of experts, myself included, and filled innumerable pages of print.

In an article entitled "Are You Too Good to Your Kids?," Martin Seligman, professor of psychology at the University of Pennsylvania, notes that self-esteem gained attention in the academic world when it became the subject of intense research. The groundbreaking work of one man firmly established that family dynamics and self-esteem are directly related. In the 1960s, Dr. Stanley Coopersmith, a professor of psychology at the University of California, devised a test for measuring self-esteem in children. He then went on to assess the child-rearing practices of the parents of the children who scored high in self-esteem. His findings were startling. The evidence for high self-esteem pointed to families in which children learned rules early, and where the rules were consistently enforced by parents. In fact, the clearer the rules, and the more consistent the enforcement, the higher the child's self-esteem. Conversely, and here's the sticky part, the greater the freedom a child was permitted, the lower his or her self-esteem seemed to be. In families with few or no rules, children apparently felt unconnected and there was fair-to-poor performance in and out of school. Well, that didn't exactly fit many people's notion of how self-esteem was formed, and a general confusion fell upon the land. Rules can't be fun! And the person enforcing rules won't be liked. Which way now for the self-esteem train to go?

Where well-intentioned folks swerved off-track was in equating the development of enhanced self-esteem with *feeling* good. The feel-good school of self-esteem became widely viewed as the answer to poor school grades, adolescent apathy, vandalism, drug and alcohol abuse, juvenile delinquency, and teenage pregnancy. What Dr. Coopersmith specifically advocated, however, didn't have very much to do with kids feeling good. On the contrary, his firm and consistent rules and their enforcement translated as discipline, which is not frequently perceived as creating good feelings. At least, not in the short term. Parents and schools, in fact, took Dr. Coopersmith's credo of discipline to mean being harsh with kids and unpopular with them. Unfortunately, those who believe that having youngsters like them is a prerequisite to fostering self-esteem are vulnerable to attitudes and behaviors that may not always be in the youngsters' best interests. But popularity won out and the feel-good movement grew deeper roots. The problem was that it didn't work.

One of the difficulties with the feel-good approach to self-esteem development lies in the fact that it is next to impossible to define self-esteem in this way, and harder still to devise effective techniques for instilling it. It's a great idea. Who wouldn't want to feel good? Good feelings, however, can't just be handed over or given to someone like a piece of candy or a pat on the back. Authentic self-esteem is built up over a period of time through numerous encounters and experiences that form thriving beliefs in ourselves as having worth, maintaining the confidence to cope with stress, sustaining the ability to meet life's challenges and to accept failure.

Another drawback is that this approach does not generate the kind of precise or meaningful technology that parents and teachers can understand and apply. It's like the Nike shoe commercial: *Just Do It!* And the small voice inside answers back: *Do what?* In the same way, it's fine to say: *Make them feel good!* On the other hand, the voice asks: *How?*

Few answers developed through the 1960s, 70s, and 80s that

proved of real value in assisting teachers, counselors, and parents to achieve the fuzzy goal of getting youngsters to feel good about themselves as a means of improving self-esteem.

To muddy the picture even further, the feel-good approach to self-esteem became equated with *doing* good. In other words, self-esteem got tagged with the notion that appreciating one's own worth and importance, and exhibiting such admirable character traits as responsibility and accountability, were the result of becoming skilled in confronting and completing tasks, working successfully, conquering frustration and boredom, and ultimately, in *winning*. And it didn't matter winning at what, or where or when—it was simply winning at anything and everything, succeeding at anything and everything.

The concept of winning permeates our society. And, in order for someone to win, someone has to lose. No matter how many times Dad, when coaching Saturday morning soccer or Little League, instructs his young players, "Just go out there and have fun. It doesn't matter if you win or lose," the kids know it's baloney. Is Dad crazy—or stupid? What coach wouldn't want his team to win? Aren't we supposed to want to win? Everybody knows winning *is* better.

The bottom line, in truth, is that self-esteem is not, and can *never* be created by doing, succeeding, or winning at anything. Doing, succeeding, and winning are *behaviors,* and therefore *external.* Authentic self-esteem—self-esteem that is a part of us from within—is fostered by what we *believe* to be fundamentally true about ourselves, and is therefore *internal.* There are many possible high esteem–generating beliefs: *I am a resourceful person; I count; I have worth; I belong; I am smart; I am good enough; I can do it; I am creative, resourceful, lovable, connected, safe, a good person; I can express my thoughts and feelings; I am valued and acknowledged; I am trustworthy, flexible; I can stand up for myself, get along with others, speak my mind.* And if, on the contrary, I don't have thriving beliefs such as these and others about myself, then, when my self-esteem is scraping the bottom of the feel-good barrel, my attitude about myself won't be altered one teensy bit by someone's attempts to make me feel good about myself, by my winning the game, or making the most sales, or having the newest car in the neighborhood. These temporary feel-goods quickly fade if underlying beliefs tell me that I'm a failure or stupid, that I have no worth, don't count, don't belong, can't connect. Winning the game does not instill the belief *I am a winner*. Making the most sales or having the newest car does not generate the belief *I am a good and valuable person*.

If authentic self-esteem is generated by our beliefs about ourselves and not by being successful or winning, and belief formation is the key to self-esteem, how are such thriving beliefs generated? How do we develop them? Beliefs are formed from our first experiences in childhood, and are the result of learning about ourselves through our relationships with others and the world around us. Research shows that even before we are born, while we are curled up tight and snug in a secure, warm place with a feeding and breathing tube and not a care in the world, many things affect our state of being. For example, the attitude of a mother and father about being parents, their feelings for each other and their attitudes towards the world all have a profound effect on that tiny, newly forming human consciousness. After we are born, every experience continues to be imprinted and literally forms impressions or traces in the brain that become a permanent part of the neural network, an extremely complex web of electrical and biochemical pathways. These pathways eventually give us the ability to walk, tie our shoelaces, eat our soup with a spoon—and retain the beliefs that are becoming an integral part of us. Take, for instance, these few examples that a child might take in, consciously or otherwise, as the foundation for newly forming beliefs: *Dad spends time with me; Mother smiles when I enter the room; my sister lets me help with the party preparations*. The time shared with the family for this youngster is very important; the experiences register and form a pathway in the brain that becomes a positive, thriving belief system: *I am a worthwhile person; I am lovable; I am capable*. Self-affirming beliefs formed in early childhood are what allow us to participate meaningfully in life and maintain states of health, well-being, satisfaction, connectedness, self-worth, and joy.

These self-affirming beliefs are the basis of self-esteem. It is only through experiences that are internalized (imprinted on the brain) that beliefs are formed. Relationships and experiences in childhood that foster these positive beliefs lead to high self-esteem, character formation, and the development of a number of important life skills. Through these self-affirming beliefs we learn the importance of *dealing* with stress rather than beating out or avoiding frustration; of *accepting* that life is filled with challenges and opportunities rather than keeping score, with winning the high priority; and of *recognizing* that difficulties, rather than heralding blunders, shortfalls or failure, can, in fact, be the doorway to self-understanding, acceptance of ourselves and others, and greater wisdom.

What does belief formation (internal) versus winning and succeeding (external) have to do with children's games? The way in which we interact as adults in our personal and business lives is fixed from the time we first walk out onto the school playground. The games we play as children establish life skills and determine the pulse of our values and standards throughout our lives. This is because the school playground is where some of the most powerful beliefs about ourselves are formed. And what goes on out there, as well as in the classroom and on the baseball and soccer fields? Winning. And competition. Competition is so carefully taught that many of us appear uncommonly grudging and uncooperative in our whole outlook on life. We are not only conditioned to compete, but also to *want* to compete, and therefore, to win. And this socialization takes place not only on the playground and in the sports arena, but in the educational system as well. From nursery school to graduate school, the notion that competition is natural, inevitable, and good is impressed upon us as an accepted fact. In the classroom, when a youngster raises his or her hand to respond to the teacher's question, how many others sit there hoping the answer will be wrong so they can give the correct one and look good in the teacher's eyes? One student's failure is a chance for another to succeed. Among the Hopi Indians and other Native American and indigenous peoples around the world, this behavior would not be acceptable. In a system that values respect and cooperation, mistakes merely call for correction.

The interesting paradox is that competition is not inevitable. As much evidence exists for cooperation as for competition. In fact, we systematically underestimate or delete from our awareness the significant role cooperation plays in our lives by the very fact that we live and work together. Our lives are profoundly interdependent, and basic human survival is based not on competition but upon cooperative interaction.

In a society that values serving and sharing, a major shift takes place. If you don't get what you want or you lose the game (or job), it's not viewed as a failure. The worst that happens is that you feel inconvenienced for a while. In a non-competitive society, this normal life experience is valued rather than avoided, because such experiences help us become clearer about ourselves and what is important to us. We like ourselves better and we become more resourceful. This builds character, which goes hand in hand with building resourceful beliefs about ourselves. So we have winners and we have learners.

Research indicates that children are very receptive to challenges in which the reward or prize is enhanced through cooperative learning, teamwork, or team play. Toddlers and even infants have a tendency to cooperate and to work actively together. Some of these cooperation-based ideas are beginning to filter into the fabric of American business, industry, and education. Today a few clear-sighted business consultants are guiding corporate executives and managers through unconventional but effective processes that involve sitting, lying, and crawling on hotel room floors. These exercises replicate what happens naturally with toddlers. When adults engage in activities they did when they were very young children—crawling, drawing, playing together—it stimulates greater creativity and cooperative team building. One of the reasons this approach works is that the crawling, drawing, and playing nudge old neural pathways so that the strangeness of doing things differently (cooperatively) is supported by recalling the behavior on some non-verbal but accessible level.

This is not to say that competitive play can't be fun, enjoyable or even educational. But in terms of the development of self-esteem or character, winning the game does not instill the belief *I am a winner*. It instills the belief *I can gain approval and acceptance by behaving in the way they expect me to.* Unfortunately, we don't learn from a strategy designed to gain another's approval or acceptance. How do we feel good about ourselves when there is no cheering crowd or someone to accept and approve of us?

What does this have to do with a book on noncompetitive children's games and activities? Well, the answer should be clear by now. The nice thing about learned behavior is that it can be unlearned. Most of the games and activities cited in Ms. Blosser's one-of-a-kind book already exist and are familiar to us in their competitive form. However, in their presentation here, the games and activities retain their structure and rules, but the non-competitive spin allows them to work wonderfully as fun-filled ways for youngsters to learn to play, participate, and cooperate—that is, learn to do things differently.

Ms. Blosser's collection of games and activities, each one accompanied by a clear set of guidelines, offers practical and applicable tools to parents, teachers, and scout leaders for important skill development and positive belief formation in young people. And enhanced self-esteem is the natural benefit—along with the building blocks of character formation. Armchair experts, whether scholastic, psychological, or parental, would do well to take note of Ms. Blosser's formula for fun, where what counts is participating with others, cooperatively and non-competitively, as an individual or in a group, in prescribed ways that are clearly spelled out and easy to follow.

What also comes through in all of these games and activities is that Ms. Blosser is a person with a great deal of hands-on experience in teaching cooperation and non-competitive fun. And she really knows her kids. Along with each game and activity are practical pointers, such as not fully inflating balloons because fat balloons pop more easily or buying gumdrops that aren't spicy, or reminders about safety, such as emptying water containers immediately after an activity, using paper bags rather than plastic, and, after a game, securing anything that could find its way into small mouths. She also offers hints about how to make the games more fun or how to modify them for success with older children.

In terms of self-esteem formation, Ms. Blosser's suggestions enable a child to build such healthy beliefs as *I can belong to a group in constructive ways; I have something of worth to contribute; I am wanted and valued; it's okay to experiment; it's okay to do it in a different way; I don't have to win to be accepted or loved; I like playing with you; I like you.* Ms. Blosser assists children to learn at an early age that it's not the doing or winning that counts, but the sharing, learning, and participating (caring) that reap the long-term rewards. WHO CARES *WINS.*

In addition to developing the skills of cooperative play, Ms. Blosser's games and activities provide a wealth of other benefits.

Some of them teach communication skills; others improve listening ability, encourage collaborative or helping behavior, team effort, and sharing. Some stimulate thinking and reasoning, creativity, and skill building, such as naming colors, counting and cutting. Many of the games and activities are also suited for children with learning differences or physical challenges. Incidentally, a crowd isn't a requirement in order to teach cooperation. Many of the games and activities can also be used by a parent and just one child.

When children, whether they are four or forty, each get a gift or prize for participating, they learn that they can meet life's challenges in optimistic, energetic, and self-assured ways, and positive self-esteem and constructive character traits grow. In other words, in Jody Blosser's world, *everybody wins!*

At the back of this book, on pages 137–141, you'll find a chart that has been prepared for you as a parent, teacher or friend of children. There are a number of points about each game or activity described in the book that may be useful to you, such as a quick reference list showing age ranges, number of players, time for preparation and playing time. It also covers belief formation, and specifies which games and activities are especially effective in teaching collaborative or helping behavior, sharing, character development, communication and listening skills; which stimulate thinking, reasoning and creativity, team effort, skill building (recognizing colors, counting, cutting); and which are particularly good to consider when you're working with children who have learning differences or physical challenges.

So, get out those safety scissors—and start having fun!

Gaylyn Larned, Ph.D
Westport, Connecticut
January 19, 1996

GAMES

I've always loved parties, and coming from a rather large family, I've been to plenty. Now, as a mother of three young children and a childcare professional operating my own home daycare, I'm the giver, not the recipient. And I still love parties! But I've learned that the best parties, at least for young children, are the ones that use non-competitive games. I learned the hard way, coping with little party guests' tears, frustration, and stress, as they struggled to compete in games that should have been fun. I know there must be thousands and thousands of adults out there who will be throwing parties for young children this year. Many of those parties will be filled with children's unhappiness and tears, simply because the adults giving them haven't yet gained the experience necessary to know which games work well with young children and which don't. That's why I wrote this book—to share with party givers some games and activities that will help ensure a party's success.

Several of the games here are great ones I played as a child. Others are traditional games that I have changed to a non-competitive format. Friends told me about some of them, and others I simply made up. I have played all the games in this book with my own children at their parties. They all place the emphasis on fun—not winning!

By the way, many of these games and activities can be enjoyed by a single child as well as in a party atmosphere, and so are great for parents, grandparents, and other adults to use at home in everyday situations.

For many of the games, prizes are optional, but I've found that children really enjoy getting and opening prizes after each game. With this in mind, I have also included a list of 100 inexpensive prize suggestions. The prizes are listed according to the ages of the children who will be receiving them. There is also a section that gives instructions for making your own party prizes—really interesting ones that kids love. If you decide to give prizes after each game, you can give the children empty goody bags as they arrive, and then, during the course of the party, they can fill the bags with their loot. I also wrap the prizes when feasible, because all kids love to unwrap presents.

I have also included a sample "guest list," which I've found very useful. This page, which can be copied for multiple use, includes spaces for the names of the guests, their ages, their phone numbers, and a response. By filling out the guest list page two to three weeks before the party, you will have at your fingertips all the information you need to help you choose the games, activities, and prizes that are right for the group.

I hope your children enjoy playing these games and taking part in these activities as much as mine do. So look through the book, make your selections, and HAVE A GREAT PARTY!

TOY FLOAT
● ● ● ● ● ● ● ● ● ● ●

THE GAME: From a selection of toys floating in a small pool or other container, children scoop one toy, read the number, and get their prize.

AGE LEVEL: 1–3

NUMBER OF PLAYERS: 4–5 per pool of water

APPROXIMATE PREPARATION TIME: 5 minutes

ESTIMATED TIME FOR GAME: 5 minutes

MATERIALS NEEDED (per pool):
- small wading pool or other container of a similar size that will hold water
- plastic toys that float—1 or 2 per child
- permanent or alcohol-based marker
- water
- prizes—all different or 3 or more each of 3 different prizes

BEFORE THE PARTY: Gather together plastic toys that will float in water without easily tipping or turning over. On the bottom of each (the side that is underwater when the toy is floating) write a number with the permanent or alcohol-based marker. If you use an alcohol-based marker, the numbers can be removed easily after the party using rubbing alcohol and a cotton ball. The numbers you need to write will depend on the prizes you are using. If all the prizes are different, write a different number on the bottom of each toy, starting with the number 1 and continuing until you have one numbered toy for each of the prizes. Draw a smiley face and write the words "Try Again" on any extra toys. If you are using several each of three different prizes, divide your floating toys into four piles, putting enough plastic toys in each of the first three piles to correspond with the prizes. For example, if you have three of prize type A, three of prize type B, and four of prize type C, place three floating toys in pile one, three floating toys in pile two, and four floating toys in pile three. Put the remaining floating toys in pile four. On the bottom of the floating toys in pile one write the number 1; on the bottom of the toys in pile two write the number 2; and on the bottom of the toys in pile three write the number 3. On the bottom of the toys in pile four, draw a smiley face and write the words "Try Again."

Next, wrap the prizes. Then, using a marker, write numbers on the wrapped prizes that correspond with the numbers on the floating toys. Right before the party starts, put several inches of water in the wading pool or other container (a bathtub works well if you are playing the game indoors) and then place the floating toys in the water, being careful to make sure they are floating so that the numbers do not show.

HOW TO PLAY: Have the children gather around the pool or tub. Then, have one child at a time reach into the water and scoop up a toy. After the child has retrieved a toy, have him turn it over to discover what number is on the bottom. The prize which matches that number is his. If the toy says "Try Again," that child gets to scoop another toy from the water. Toys that have been scooped from the water are *not* returned to the water, but rather set aside. The game continues until everyone has a prize.

To add challenge to this game for older children, have them scoop the toys from the water using a butterfly net, a soup ladle, or any other object that can be used like a scoop.

HELPFUL HINTS:
- Watch children carefully around the water before, during, and after this game. Children can easily trip and fall into the water while playing and get hurt. Or they may just decide to climb into the water.
- As soon as the game is finished, dump the water from the container and set the container aside.
- If you do not wish to wrap the prizes, you can number slips of paper and tape them to the prizes.

BALLOON HUNT

THE GAME: An easy game for very young children, similar to an Easter egg hunt. The children hunt for balloons and keep the ones they find.

AGE LEVEL: 1–3

NUMBER OF PLAYERS: 4–unlimited, depending upon space

APPROXIMATE PREPARATION TIME: 15 minutes

ESTIMATED TIME FOR GAME: 10 minutes

MATERIALS NEEDED:
- balloons—at least 4 per player (smaller balloons work best)
- bags to hold balloons—1 per player

BEFORE THE PARTY: Blow up all the balloons. For best results, do not fully inflate the balloons. Fully inflated balloons tend to pop rather easily. Hide the balloons in locations where a small child can easily discover them. This game can be played indoors or out.

HOW TO PLAY: The object of the game is for each player to find as many balloons as possible. Give each child a bag with his/her name on it. Paper bags are safer than plastic bags, but if all the parents are with their children, you may want to use plastic grocery bags, which are nice because they have handles. All the balloons the players find are theirs to keep.

HELPFUL HINTS:
- As always when using balloons, do not leave any uninflated balloons or pieces of popped ballons lying around, because they may find their way into a young child's or pet's mouth and are very easy to choke on.
- If you do use plastic bags, watch carefully that the children don't put them over their head or around their mouth. These things could cause suffocation.

FISHING FOR TREASURE

THE GAME: Children use a homemade fishing pole with a magnet on the end to catch a paper fish and get a prize.

AGE LEVEL: 2–8

NUMBER OF PLAYERS: 1–12 per fish pond

APPROXIMATE PREPARATION TIME: 20 minutes (makes two fishing poles that children will share)

ESTIMATED TIME FOR GAME: 3 minutes per child

MATERIALS NEEDED:
- unsharpened pencil—1 per fishing pole
- yarn—one 24″ (60 cm) length per fishing pole
- small but strong magnets—1 per fishing pole
- hot glue gun
- construction paper—enough to make at least one fish per child
- pattern for making fish (page 122)
- paper clips—1 per fish
- black or dark marker
- a variety of prizes—1 per fish
- 2″ (5 cm) squares of paper—1 per prize
- masking tape or a small bluish-colored blanket

BEFORE THE PARTY: Using the pattern on page 122 or one of your own and some construction paper, trace and cut out enough fish so that you will have at least one per party guest. It's a good idea to have at least one or two extra fish for this game, but not necessary. After cutting out the fish, write a number on the back beginning with number 1 and continuing until each fish has a number.

Next, place a paper clip over the nose end of the fish in the area indicated on the pattern. The fish are now ready to use. To make the fishing pole, tie one end of the piece of yarn to the eraser end of the unsharpened pencil. Next, hot-glue the other end of the yarn to the back of the magnet. Let the glue harden; then test the strength of the magnet by placing one fish on the floor and trying to "catch it." To do this, you must touch the

18

magnet from the pole to the paper clip on the fish. If the magnet is strong enough, you will be able to pick up the fish. If it doesn't work, you need to find stronger magnets. Make as many poles as you wish—generally, about one pole for every three to four children.

After the pole(s) and fish are ready, prepare the prizes. First, take the 2″ squares of paper and write a number on each, starting with 1 and continuing until you have a numbered square for each prize. Wrap the prizes and then tape one numbered square onto each, making sure the numbers are easy to see. Just before the party starts, make the "fish pond." To do this, outline a large circle on the floor with masking tape, or spread out a small bluish-colored blanket to act as the fish pond.

HOW TO PLAY: Divide the children into groups, one group per fishing pole, and have them stand around the "pond." Place the fish in the pond with the numbered sides down. Show the children how to catch a fish by demonstrating with one of the poles. Decide who will get to fish first in each group (perhaps the youngest or oldest, or maybe the shortest or tallest, or however you want to decide) and give each of those children a fishing pole. Each child will get to catch one fish. Then they remove it from the hook (magnet) and give their pole to the next child. Each child should keep his/her fish until everyone is done fishing. Then everyone should match the number on the fish with the numbered prizes. The prize with the corresponding number is theirs.

HELPFUL HINTS:
- Blue is just the suggested color for the blanket. You can also use other colors.
- If you cover the fish with clear contact paper or laminate them, they will last through many hours of "fishing."
- You can also use this game to help teach colors, using several colors of construction paper. As the children catch the fish, you tell them the colors. As they get older, they can tell you the colors.

THE INCREDIBLE SHRINKING PRIZE
• • • • • • • • • • • • • • • • • • • •

THE GAME: Children pass a box around, stopping when the music stops and unwrapping the outer box to reveal a smaller wrapped box inside until they reach the prizes.

AGE LEVEL: 2–8

NUMBER OF PLAYERS: 3–8 per circle

APPROXIMATE PREPARATION TIME: 30 minutes

ESTIMATED TIME FOR GAME: 10 minutes

MATERIALS NEEDED:
- nesting boxes (boxes that fit inside each other)—as many as the number of guests you will have. The more guests, the more boxes you will need. You can use plastic or paper grocery bags in place of some of the boxes and create a layering effect.
- prizes—1 per child (small enough so all the prizes fit into the smallest box)
- wrapping paper
- music (cassette player or radio)

BEFORE THE PARTY: First, wrap all the prizes individually and put them into the smallest box. Then wrap the small box. Put the small box inside the next largest box and wrap that. Put that inside the next largest and wrap it. Continue until all the boxes (and bags if you're using them) have been nested and wrapped.

HOW TO PLAY: To play this game, have all the children sit in a circle and give one of them the large wrapped box. Start the music and have the children pass the box around and around while the music plays. After about 30 seconds, stop the music. Whoever is holding the box when the music stops gets to unwrap the first layer. Inside is another wrapped box. Start the music again and continue the game until the last box is unwrapped. If the music stops on a child who has already unwrapped a layer, that child gets to pick anyone who hasn't to take a turn. Unwrapping the last box will reveal the prizes, which are also wrapped. The child holding the box takes one prize and passes the box around so that each child can take a prize.

HELPFUL HINT:

- This game works best with smaller groups (about five or six children each), so if you have a lot of players, you may wish to divide them into smaller groups, with a set of nesting boxes for each group. All the groups can play at the same time, but you might need help monitoring them if there is more than one group.

DINOSAUR BONES

THE GAME: Guests hunt for "dinosaur bones" and then use them to create their own dinosaurs.

AGE LEVEL: 2–8

NUMBER OF PLAYERS: 1–8

APPROXIMATE PREPARATION TIME: 10 minutes

ESTIMATED TIME FOR GAME: 30–45 minutes

MATERIALS NEEDED:
- bone-shaped dog biscuits:
- 1 box small bones
- 1 box medium bones
- 1 or 2 boxes large bones
- lunch bag—1 per child
- construction paper
- school glue
- cotton swabs
- crayons
- prizes (optional)—1 for each child

BEFORE THE PARTY: "Bury" all the dog biscuits, either in your yard or, if the game cannot be played outside, in one room of your house. For younger children, it works best to just toss the bones around the yard (or room) for them to find. For older children, it is much more fun to bury the bones in a large sandbox or under other toys in the area. After burying the bones, put a guest's name on each lunch bag. Be sure to keep some of the bones in reserve in case someone does not find any.

HOW TO PLAY: The object of this game is to find as many dinosaur bones as possible and then have fun using them to make a dinosaur. It is best played outdoors and is a good game for using up excessive energy. To play, give each child a lunch bag with his/her name on it. Have the children hunt for the bones. You may wish to set a time limit of five to ten minutes. As the kids find the bones, have them put them in their bags.

When they are through hunting, have everyone sit down at a table. Give each child construction paper, glue, and crayons to make their very own dinosaur from the bones they found. When passing out the glue, give each child a small amount on a square of cardboard or in an egg cup or old medicine measuring cup with a cotton swab for spreading it. If necessary, give anyone who did not find any bones the ones from your reserve, so they can participate in the picture-making fun.

HELPFUL HINTS:
- Watch younger children carefully—they just might decide their dinos look good enough to eat!—and dog biscuits, although non-toxic, are easy to choke on.
- If you want to give prizes, wait until all the children have finished making their dinosaurs, and then pass out a prize to each child.
- For more fun, you can award the prizes for: most bones used in picture, least bones used, funniest dinosaur, biggest dinosaur, most colorful, etc. If you do this, be sure every child gets an award.

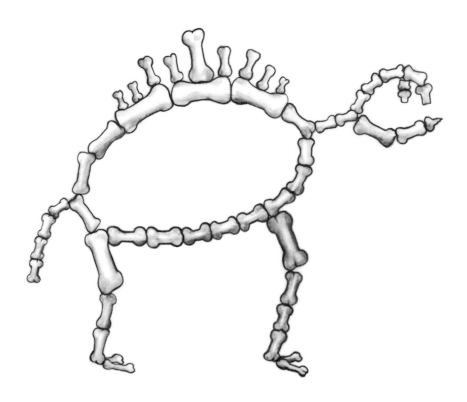

GOLD DIGGER

• • • • • • • • • • • • • • •

THE GAME: "Gold miners" dig for "gold" in a pile of sand or sawdust.

AGE LEVEL: 2–10

NUMBER OF PLAYERS: 1–8 per gold mine

APPROXIMATE PREPARATION TIME: 10 minutes

ESTIMATED TIME FOR GAME: 5 minutes

MATERIALS NEEDED (for each gold mine):
- fine sawdust or clean sandbox sand—enough to make a large pile
- a large box, wastebasket, or other container
- large plastic sheet
- pennies—about 200
- reserve supply—about 15 pennies
- plastic sandwich bag for each guest
- prizes (optional)—1 for each child

BEFORE THE PARTY: Pour the sand or sawdust into the box, wastebasket, or other container and bury the pennies in it. Write a guest's name on each sandwich bag. Set aside the small reserve of pennies.

HOW TO PLAY: The object of the game is to find as many pennies as possible. Spread a plastic sheet on the floor where you want to play the game. Pour the sawdust or sand out in the middle of the sheet. This is your gold mine. Have the children sit in a circle around it. Give each child the sandwich bag with his/her name on it. Tell them that when you say "Dig!" they will have five minutes to find as many pennies as they can and put them in their sandwich bag (you may want to use a timer, if you have one). Then say "Dig!" and let them go at it. Monitor the game so that no child gets too rough or rowdy.

When the five minutes are over, stop the game. The children keep the pennies they have found. If a child did not find any pennies, tell all the players to dig for a few pennies for that child. If this still fails to provide a player with pennies, donate a few pennies from your reserve supply. If you are using prizes, each child can buy a prize for one penny after the game is over.

HELPFUL HINTS:
- Watch small children carefully to make sure they do not put the coins in their mouths.
- If you are using sand, be sure to use clean sandbox sand to avoid small bits of gravel that might hurt the players.
- You can buy sandbox sand from a gravel company or in bags at most hardware stores that have a garden department.
- You can get sawdust from most lumberyards. Some will even give it to you free.
- When the party is over, you can add the sawdust to your compost heap, if you have one.
- This game works best if you make a separate gold mine for every 6–8 children.

BOB-A-DOUGHNUT

THE GAME: Without hands, each party guest tries to eat a doughnut that is hanging by a string from the ceiling.

AGE LEVEL: 2–10 (2- and 3-year-olds will probably try to use their hands, but they still enjoy playing this game)

NUMBER OF PLAYERS: 1–8 per cord

APPROXIMATE PREPARATION TIME: 15 minutes

ESTIMATED TIME FOR GAME: 10 minutes

MATERIALS NEEDED:
- doughnuts with a hole in the center—1 for each guest plus extras in case some break
- cord
- string or yarn
- several clothespins
- several clean plastic grocery or freezer bags
- prizes (optional). The doughnuts are usually the prize, but if you decide to reward the players for a job well done, wait

to award the prizes until all the children have finished playing.

BEFORE THE PARTY: First decide where you want to play this game, keeping in mind that it can get messy. Now, tie or tack up a length of cord running across the playing area. It should be as high up as possible. If you use tacks to hold the cord, make sure they are pushed securely into a door frame or wall, so that they don't pop out and hit someone during the game. Next, tie each doughnut to a piece of string about three feet (1 m) long (long enough to hang from the cord to the mouth level of the children). Secure the strung doughnuts to the cord.

To keep the doughnuts fresh and clean and out of reach until game time, pull two or three strings together, tie a clean plastic bag around the doughnuts, and use a clothespin to hook the bag to the overhead cord. Repeat this with the remaining doughnuts, being careful not to crush them, because they crack and break rather easily and will fall off the string.

HOW TO PLAY: The object of the game is to eat the doughnut off the string without using your hands. Carefully remove the doughnuts from the plastic bags in which they've been kept out of reach, and let them hang, checking each one quickly to make sure it's still secure. If necessary, replace any cracked or broken ones. Have each player stand by one doughnut with hands clasped behind his/her back. As you give the doughnuts a gentle swing, the children try to eat them off the string without using their hands.

HELPFUL HINTS:
- This can get messy, so don't be surprised to find a lot of doughnut crumbs on the floor when the game is finished. It might be a good idea not to play this game over carpeting.
- Spreading old newspapers under the playing surface makes it easier to clean up the mess when the game is finished.
- If you award prizes, wrap them tightly. While the children are unwrapping them, you'll have a couple of minutes to sweep up the crumbs.

POP-A-LOONY

THE GAME: Each child takes a turn popping a balloon so that everyone can then perform the loony action described on a note inside it.

AGE LEVEL: 3–8

NUMBER OF PLAYERS: 3–12

APPROXIMATE PREPARATION TIME: 20 minutes

ESTIMATED TIME FOR GAME: 15 minutes

MATERIALS NEEDED:
- balloons—1 or 2 for each guest
- small slip of paper—approximately ½″ × 4″ (1.25 × 10 cm)—for each balloon
- string or yarn
- cellophane tape
- prizes (optional)—1 for each child

BEFORE THE PARTY: Write a simple "loony" action on each slip of paper. (See examples below.) Place each slip of paper in a balloon, blow up and tie the balloons, attach a string to each one, and tape them up around the room to curtains, ceiling, and furniture. (They'll serve as party decorations until you're ready to play the game.)

EXAMPLES OF LOONY ACTIONS:

Spin around three times while standing on one foot.

Hop on your left foot for five seconds.

Close your eyes and walk backwards.

Sing a silly song. (You might want to write the name of a silly song on the paper.)

Act like a monkey eating a banana (or any other animal doing some action).

HOW TO PLAY: The object of the game is to have fun acting loony. Have one child take a balloon and stomp it with his foot to pop it. Then have all the children act out the loony action described on the note that was inside the balloon. When they are done, another child will pick a balloon, pop it, and then everyone will act out the action described. Play will continue in this manner until everyone has had a turn to pop a balloon. Try to get the kids to act as loony as possible—the loonier the better. If you are using prizes for this game, pass them out after all the players have had a turn to pop a balloon.

HELPFUL HINTS:

- Take extra care to pick up all the popped balloon pieces so that no small guests or pets choke on them.
- To make it easier to find the slips of paper when popping the balloons, place the balloons in a plastic shopping bag before popping them.

BABY HUEY

• • • • • • • • • • • •

THE GAME: Children pretend they are babies and drink from baby bottles until the bottles are empty.

AGE LEVEL: 3–8 (younger kids can play this, but they might not really understand why everyone is acting like babies)

NUMBER OF PLAYERS: 2–any number can play

APPROXIMATE PREPARATION TIME: 5 minutes

ESTIMATED TIME FOR GAME: 10 minutes

MATERIALS NEEDED:
- baby bottles—1 for each party guest
- juice or a drink to fill the bottles
- optional: 1 baby blanket for each child, 1 or more baby rattles and other toys for each child
- prizes (optional)—1 for each child

BEFORE THE PARTY: Fill the bottles, cap them with the nipples so they are ready to use, and place in the refrigerator until game time. If using the optional blankets and rattles, have them all together as well. If using the option of prizes, pass them out after the children are finished with their bottles.

HOW TO PLAY: The object of the game is to have fun doing baby things. Give each child a baby bottle and have them drink until their bottle is empty. To add a little more fun to the party, give each player a rattle to hold and a baby blanket to lie on while drinking from the bottle. Tell the kids that if they want to move they can only crawl or scoot, and if they want to talk to each other, they can only babble in "baby talk." Remind the kids that this is not a race to see who finishes first, but just a game for acting silly.

HELPFUL HINT: When the game is over, be sure the bottles are put away in the sink so the children don't "share" germs.

BUBBLE MANIA

● ● ● ● ● ● ● ● ● ● ● ● ● ● ● ●

THE GAME: Children have fun blowing bubbles until their bubble machine is empty, thereby uncovering a prize number.

AGE LEVEL: 3–8

NUMBER OF PLAYERS: any number can play

APPROXIMATE PREPARATION TIME: 10 minutes per bubble machine

ESTIMATED TIME FOR GAME: 10 minutes

MATERIALS NEEDED:
- bubble machines—1 per child (instructions on page 111)
- white or light-colored nail polish
- dark-colored liquid tempera paint (dark blue or purple works well)—1 tsp. for each 4 ounces (120 ml) of bubbles
- bubble solution—one 4-ounce (120 ml) bottle for every 4 bubble machines
- a variety of prizes—1 per child
- small squares of paper—1 per prize
- tape

BEFORE THE PARTY: Make one bubble machine for each player, using the instructions found on page 111. Do not add the bubble solution. Instead, remove the lids from the bubble machines and paint a number on the inside bottom of each machine with the white or light-colored nail polish. Start with number 1 inside the first bubble machine, then 2 inside the next one, and so on, continuing until each bubble machine has a number in it. Let the nail polish dry completely.

While the polish is drying, add one teaspoon of dark-colored liquid tempera paint to every 4 ounces (120 ml) of bubble solution. Mix well and set aside.

Wrap the presents. Write numbers on the squares of paper to correspond with the numbers inside the bubble machines. Tape one square of paper to each prize.

Just before the party starts, stir the bubble solution and then pour about ½ inch of the solution into each bubble machine and put the lids back on.

HOW TO PLAY: This is an outdoor game. Have the children gather around you so that everyone can see you. Show the children one of the bubble machines and explain to them how they work. When you blow through the straw that's in the hole on one side of the lid, the bubbles spill out of the hole that's on the other side of the lid. Tell the children that they will each be given a bubble machine and that they will need to blow bubbles until their bubble solution is gone. Explain to them that when their bubble solution is all gone they can remove the lid, and find their number. The number in each child's bubble machine will dictate which prize the child wins. After explaining the game to the children, give each child a bubble machine and let them have fun.

HELPFUL HINTS:

- Children under 3 should not be given bubble machines, because they tend to use the straw to drink the bubble solution as opposed to blowing bubbles with it.
- Remind the children to be careful when moving about during and after this game, because bubbles can make the ground slippery.
- The bubble machines can be given to the children to keep as an additional prize when the game is over.

MIDNIGHT PRIZES
• • • • • • • • • • • • • • • • • • • •

THE GAME: Children use flashlights to find prizes wrapped in foil and hidden throughout a dark room.

AGE LEVEL: 3–8

NUMBER OF PLAYERS: 1–12

APPROXIMATE PREPARATION TIME: 10 minutes

ESTIMATED TIME FOR GAME: 5 minutes

MATERIALS NEEDED:
- flashlights—3 or 4
- foil
- prizes—1 per child

BEFORE THE PARTY: First, make sure the flashlights have good batteries in them. Then, wrap all the prizes in foil making sure that the shiniest side is facing out. Even if the prizes are small, wrap the foil large so that the flashlights have a large surface to reflect from. Next, hide all of the prizes in a room which, when the lights are turned off, is very dark. A room with no windows, such as a basement, works well.

HOW TO PLAY: When it is time to start this game, have the children gather around. Explain to them that they will go into a dark room and use their flashlights to find their prizes, which are wrapped in foil. The foil on the prizes will shine just a little when light is aimed at it. Have the children go into the dark room two or three at a time to find their "midnight prizes." If too many children go in at one time, the flashlights tend to light up the room, taking the fun out of prize hunting in the dark.

HELPFUL HINTS:
- Remember to keep the ages of the children in mind when hiding the prizes. For younger children, you can just lay the prizes around the room. For older children, you can hide the prizes in more challenging places.
- If you do not have a large enough room that is also dark, you can cover the windows with blankets, or wait until it is dark outside.

- If you do not have enough flashlights, you can ask each of the party guests to bring one from home. The children who bring flashlights can share theirs with anyone who forgets or does not have one to bring.
- Never force a child to go into the dark room. Some children are genuinely afraid of the dark. You might offer to go with a child who is frightened, but if that doesn't work, just ask one of the other children to help out by finding an extra prize to give to the child who does not want to go.

CRAZY CRITTERS

THE GAME: Children pass pictures of different animal parts around a circle to the sound of music. After all parts have been passed out, children glue the three parts they ended up with together to form a "crazy critter" to color and name.

AGE LEVEL: 3–10

NUMBER OF PLAYERS: 3–15

APPROXIMATE PREPARATION TIME: 10 minutes

ESTIMATED TIME FOR GAME: 15 minutes

MATERIALS NEEDED:
- copies of 3-part crazy critter patterns (see page 123–132)— 1 per child
- scissors
- cassette player and cassette or other source of music
- sheets of construction paper—1 piece per child
- glue
- clean medicine dosage cups (the kind that come free with some medications)—1 per child
- cotton swabs—1 per child
- crayons
- prizes (optional)—1 per child

BEFORE THE PARTY: Cut apart the 3-part crazy critter patterns on the dotted lines and fold each piece in half. Divide the folded parts into three piles: one for heads, one for middles, and one for feet. Gather together the rest of your supplies.

HOW TO PLAY: Have the children sit in a circle on the floor. Give each child one folded head piece. Explain that they will be passing the pieces around the circle while listening to music. When the music stops, the children place the head piece they are holding on the floor in front of them. Next, pass out the middle body pieces. Again, have the children pass the pieces around to the sound of music. When the music stops, they place their middle body piece on the floor with their head piece. Then, hand out the feet pieces for the children to pass around to the sound of music. When the music stops, everyone will have all three pieces with which to make their crazy critter.

Have the children take their crazy critter pieces to the table. Give each child one piece of construction paper, one medicine cup with about a quarter of an inch of glue in it, and one cotton swab. The children can then glue their crazy critters together on their construction paper and color them. Get the children to come up with crazy names for their crazy critters. If you wish to give out prizes for this game, make up awards to go with the prizes. The awards can say things such as: silliest critter, most colorful critter, craziest critter, zaniest critter, weirdest critter, etc. Make sure that every child receives an award.

HELPFUL HINTS:
- There are ten crazy critter patterns at the back of this book. Even if you have fewer than ten children playing this game, you can use parts from all ten patterns. If you have more than ten, you can use duplicate copies of some of the animals.
- It is best to copy the crazy critter patterns at the back of the book, retaining the originals. That way the game can be played over and over.

ANCIENT TREASURE DIG

THE GAME: Children sift through sand or sawdust to find as many "ancient gems" as they can. Then the children clean their gems by chipping and rubbing off the coating of sediment that is covering them (from years of being buried, of course).

AGE LEVEL: 3–10

NUMBER OF PLAYERS: 1–6 per dig pile

APPROXIMATE PREPARATION TIME: 30 minutes (not counting drying time for plaster of Paris)

ESTIMATED TIME FOR GAME: 20 minutes

MATERIALS NEEDED (per dig pile):
- medium-sized plastic gems—about 10 per child
- plaster of Paris—1 cup for every 75 gems
- water—½ cup for every 75 gems
- 2 disposable 9-ounce (270 ml) plastic cups (use larger disposable containers if you are using more than 75 gems)
- tweezers
- foil
- food coloring (optional)
- fine sawdust or clean sandbox sand—in one big pile
- a large, clean trash can or other container large enough to hold the sand or sawdust until you are ready to use it
- a large plastic sheet or a double-size or larger bed sheet
- plastic sandwich bags—1 per child

BEFORE THE PARTY: First, prepare the gems. This needs to be done *at least* 24 hours before the party. Begin by mixing half the plaster of Paris with half the water in one of the disposable 9-ounce cups (or larger containers, if necessary) according to the directions on the plaster of Paris box. Lay a piece of foil big enough to hold all the gems on a flat surface such as a counter or table. Using the tweezers, dip the gems, one at a time, into the prepared plaster and then place them on the foil to dry. After at least one hour, prepare the remaining plaster of Paris and re-dip the gems, being careful to lay them on a different side to dry. If you wish to have colored ancient treasure, add

35

food coloring to the second batch of plaster of Paris before re-dipping the gems. Let the gems dry for at least 24 hours.

After the gems have completely dried, set aside one gem to show to the children at game time, and mix the remaining gems into the container of sand or sawdust.

HOW TO PLAY: When it is time to start the game, spread out a large plastic or old cotton bed sheet on a relatively flat surface. Dump the sand or sawdust (with the ancient treasure already mixed in) onto the sheet. Have the children gather around. Give each child a sandwich bag. Show the children the ancient gem that you set aside earlier so that they will know what to look for. Tell the children they will have ten minutes to "dig up" as many ancient treasures as they can find. As they find the treasures, the children put them in their sandwich bags.

After about ten minutes, stop the "treasure dig." Have the children gather around a table to "clean up" their treasures. Show the children how to clean the sediment (plaster of Paris) off their gems. This is done by pinching and rubbing the ancient treasure between your fingers, thereby breaking the plaster away. When everyone has finished cleaning their treasure, it goes back in their sandwich bags to take home as their prize, or you can have the children make a jeweled crown with their findings. Directions for jeweled crowns are on page 77.

HELPFUL HINTS:
- You can purchase clean sand at most large hardware stores.
- You can get sawdust from most lumberyards. Some will even give it to you free of charge. If you use sawdust, check it carefully for small splinters of wood and any other items that might harm the children.
- You can buy plastic gems at most craft stores.
- If you cannot find any plastic gems, you can use colorful plastic beads.
- If you plan to follow this game with the Jeweled Crown activity on page 77, it is best to use gems with at least one flat side.
- If any children have trouble cracking and chipping the plaster off their gems, you can get them started by tapping their gems with the handle end of a butter knife, screwdriver, or other similar object.

PENNY POTS

THE GAME: Players attempt to toss pennies and other coins into "penny pots." When a player gets his/her coin in the pot, he/she wins the prize attached to that penny pot.

AGE LEVEL: 3–12

NUMBER OF PLAYERS: 1–16

APPROXIMATE PREPARATION TIME: 15 minutes

ESTIMATED TIME FOR GAME: 15 minutes

MATERIALS NEEDED:
- pennies and other coins—about 10 of each type (play money or chips can also be used)
- sturdy cups—1 per player plus 3 or 4 extras
- rubber bands—1 per cup
- assorted prizes—1 per cup
- masking tape

BEFORE THE PARTY: Use the rubber bands to attach one un-wrapped prize to the outside of each cup. (If the cup is shaped so that the rubber band will not attach the prize to the cup, place the prize in the cup or under it.) Using the masking tape, make a square on the floor, at least three feet (1 m) square (see hint below). Place all the cups with prizes attached in the middle of the square. Another way of setting this game up—outside—is to use four stakes set up in a square with rope tied around them.

HOW TO PLAY: The object of the game is to win a prize by tossing a coin into a penny pot (sturdy cup). Four children play

at a time. Give each player a handful of coins (each one should get a different denomination) and have each child stand on a different side of the square. All the players try tossing their coins, one at a time, into the penny pots in the middle of the square. Once they land a coin in a pot, they win the pot prize. If any players run out of coins before winning a prize, give them back the coins so they can keep trying. As each player wins a prize, another player takes a turn until every player has won.

HELPFUL HINTS:

- The size of the square will depend upon the age of the players. The three-foot (1 m) square is appropriate for smaller children, but older children will require a larger square.
- Remind the players not to throw their coins too hard, because they might hit a player on another side of the square.

RING AROUND THE REINDEER

THE GAME: Children toss plastic bracelets at clothespin reindeer standing on a board. When they ring a reindeer, they get a prize.

AGE LEVEL: 3–12

NUMBER OF PLAYERS: 1–10

APPROXIMATE PREPARATION TIME: 20 minutes

ESTIMATED TIME FOR GAME: 10 minutes

MATERIALS NEEDED:
- 6 average-size craft clothespins (not the type with springs in them)
- 6 wiggle eyes
- a 2″ × 4″ (5 × 10 cm) block of wood approximately 6 inches (15 cm) long
- brown tempera paint
- 3 extra-small fuzzy balls—each one a different color
- a hot glue gun
- a flat surface, such as a small table that is about waist high to the children
- plastic bracelets—5–10
- a variety of prizes—generally three or four prizes of each type, with a different type for each reindeer—making sure that there are enough prizes for every child with a few left over
- 3 slips of paper—approximately 2″ × 2″ (5 × 5 cm)
- 3 markers or crayons that correspond to the colors of the fuzzy balls

BEFORE THE PARTY: For this game you need to make three reindeer from clothespins. Begin by painting the clothespins brown. When the paint has dried, hot glue the clothespins together to form a reindeer as shown in the illustration. Then hot glue the eyes in place, followed by the fuzzy ball nose. When the hot glue has cooled off sufficiently, hot glue the reindeer to the piece of wood.

Place the small table in the area where the game will be played.

Place the reindeer on it. Make a circle or other mark on each slip of paper using a marker of the same color as the fuzzy ball nose on the reindeer—one slip for each reindeer.

Wrap the prizes. Put the prizes into piles, one type of prize for each pile, one pile for each reindeer. Place the slips of paper on the prize piles so that each pile corresponds to a reindeer. Use the masking tape to make a throw line on the floor about four feet (122 cm) from the table. Gather together five to ten plastic bracelets to use as throwing rings.

HOW TO PLAY: Have the children line up behind the throw line. Hand the first child the stack of bracelets. If the child rings a reindeer with one of the bracelets, the child gets a prize from the corresponding pile of prizes. If the child does not ring a reindeer, he/she goes to the end of the line to try again. Continue in this manner until everyone has had a turn. Any children who have to throw a second time move forward two steps before throwing. If any children have to throw a third time, they move forward three steps, etc., until everyone is finally able to ring a reindeer and get a prize.

HELPFUL HINTS:
- You can simplify this game by making all the prizes the same, but it is still fun to have different-colored reindeer.
- If a child gets upset because he has to go to the end of the line, let the child step forward and throw again, stepping closer with each throw until a reindeer is rung. If you do this for one child, continue to do it for the rest.

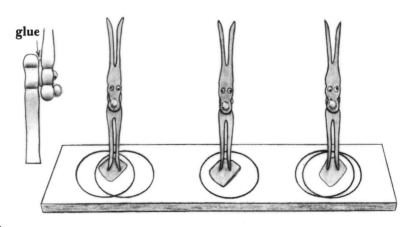

BALLOON BELLIES

THE GAME: In this game, each player searches for a balloon that contains in its "belly" an object that matches a picture given to the player.

AGE LEVEL: 4–8

NUMBER OF PLAYERS: 1–15

APPROXIMATE PREPARATION TIME: 15 minutes (if using pictures in this book)

ESTIMATED TIME FOR GAME: 15 minutes

MATERIALS NEEDED:
- balloons—at least 2 per player
- small objects to put inside balloons—1 per balloon, each one different (see suggestions below)
- plastic grocery bag
- cellophane tape
- string or yarn
- pictures of some of the objects above (you can use the ones on page 133 or draw your own)—1 per player (there will be extra balloons with no pictures to match)
- index cards—1 per player
- prizes—1 per player

BEFORE THE PARTY: Place one small object in each balloon. Blow up the balloons, tie them, and tape them up around the room from curtains, ceiling, and furniture. If you are using the pictures from the pattern section, trace on another sheet of paper the ones that match the items you placed in the balloons. Cut them out and glue them onto the index cards, one picture per card. If you are drawing your own pictures, draw them right onto the index cards. You need enough picture cards so that each player will get one. There should also be some balloons that do not have a matching picture card.

SUGGESTIONS FOR OBJECTS TO PLACE IN BALLOON "BELLIES": A short pencil; another balloon; a coin; a small ball or marble; a ring; a string of beads; a bracelet or necklace; a button; a safety pin; a paper clip; a rubber band; a small race car; a jingle bell; a ponytail holder; a clothespin; a straw—anything easily recognizable through the balloon so the player doesn't mistake the wrong balloon for his/hers. Also you will need pictures of some of the objects (one per player), which might influence your selection of objects. You'll find pictures of several of these items on page 133 that you can trace, cut out, and glue to index cards.

HOW TO PLAY: The object of the game is to find the balloon that matches the picture on the card. Give the children each a picture card and tell them they should find the balloon with an item in its belly that matches the picture and bring the balloon back to the starting point. Any other balloons they find they need to leave alone. The players then begin the search. When they find their "balloon belly," they bring it back and wait for everyone to finish. When all the players have their balloons, they take turns putting them in a plastic grocery bag and stomping them with their feet to pop them.

IMPORTANT: Before you pop a balloon, place it in a plastic grocery bag. If you don't, the object in the balloon's belly might go flying wildly when the balloon is popped and someone could get seriously hurt. After each balloon is popped, check the object inside to see if it matches the child's picture card. If so, the child gets a prize. If not, the child needs to keep looking for the correct balloon belly. If any children want help, others who already have their prize can help them search.

HELPFUL HINTS:
- Take extra care to pick up all the popped balloon pieces so that no small guests or pets choke on them.
- For younger children, use light-colored balloons, which are easier to see through. However, light-colored balloons are not a necessity, as I have played this game for a Halloween party using black balloons, and the children were able to find their objects just fine.

CHALK UP A PRIZE

THE GAME: Children follow a winding chalk trail that weaves over, under, and around other chalk lines, to reach a prize at the end of the trail.

AGE LEVEL: 4–8

NUMBER OF PLAYERS: 3–8

APPROXIMATE PREPARATION TIME: 15 minutes

ESTIMATED TIME FOR GAME: 10 minutes

MATERIALS NEEDED:
- sidewalk chalk—2 different colors for each child
- 1 black or dark-colored marker
- prizes—1 per child

BEFORE THE PARTY: To play this game you need a large concrete playing surface, such as a basement floor, driveway, or patio. Before the party begins, wrap all the prizes and number them 1, 2, 3, etc., on the back using a black or other dark-colored marker. Next, depending on the number of expected guests, write the numbers 1, 2, 3, etc., on one side of the concrete area with the chalk. Use a different color for each number. Now, with the chalk, draw a line starting from each number, using the same color for the line that you used for the number. Have the different lines circle around, cross over, and pass under the other lines you are drawing, and come to an end at the other side of your play surface (not in the same order as they began). As you draw the lines, change the color of each line at least once so that the kids can't just look to the other end of the game area and know which prize is theirs. At the end of each line place the prize that corresponds to the number at the beginning.

HOW TO PLAY: The object of the game is to reach a prize by following a winding chalk trail. Have each child pick one color of chalk and stand at the numbered starting point for that line. Then the children must follow the path of their chalk colors until reaching a prize at the other end. Be sure to let the children know that their line will change color. As the children reach their prize, they should check to make sure the number on the back of the prize is the same as the number they started on. If it is, they may open the prize; if the number is not the same, they have to go back and follow the path again, hopefully with better luck. It may become necessary to help a child follow the path correctly.

HELPFUL HINTS:

- Use discretion in weaving a trail. Too many small or tight curves are very hard to follow.
- If playing indoors, avoid danger to the children or furnishings by drawing your lines only in open areas.
- Make it a point to stay away from breakable objects, sharp or protruding points, heights or other opportunities to fall, impossible obstacles, etc.
- Test all the chalk trails by making a trial run on each one.
- A word of caution: you can't play this game outside on a rainy day, because rain will wash away the chalk lines.

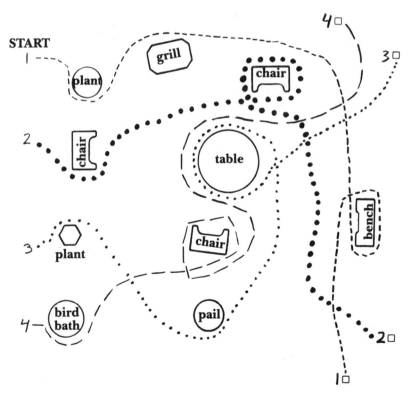

SCAVENGER HUNT

THE GAME: Find the hidden clues and follow them to find the treasure.

AGE LEVEL: 4–8

NUMBER OF PLAYERS: 1–8

APPROXIMATE PREPARATION TIME: 35 minutes

ESTIMATED TIME FOR GAME: 15 minutes

MATERIALS NEEDED:
- 3×5 index cards—5 per player. For younger children (under age 6) use colored index cards, a different color for each player, so the children won't get their cards mixed up while playing the game.
- small pictures of things in your home cut from magazines, catalogs, and store ads (no two alike; see suggestions below)—4 per player
- prizes—1 small (3×5 size) prize per player
- roll of cellophane tape

BEFORE THE PARTY: Glue the pictures onto the index cards (one picture on each card, four cards per player). Stack the picture cards in piles of four, one stack per player. Next, tape the small wrapped prize to a fifth card for each player and add that prize card to each stack. Finally, number the cards in each stack 1 through 5, making the prize card Number 5. Print the player's name on the Number 1 card in each stack.

Taking one stack of cards at a time, hide the cards around the house in this manner: Let's say the picture on Card 1 is a telephone. Tape Card 2 to a telephone with the picture down. Let's say Card 2 pictures a rocking chair. Tape Card 3 to the rocking chair with the picture down. Tape Card 4 to whatever object Card 3 depicts, and tape Card 5 to whatever object Card 4 depicts. Do this with each pile of cards.

HOW TO PLAY: The object of the game is to follow a trail of clues to find a treasure. Give each child the Number 1 card from his/her stack, the one with the name on it. Tell the players to look at the picture on the card and go to that item in the house.

There they will find another card with another picture clue, which will lead them to another card with another picture clue, until they find the treasure. Bring the treasure back to the "prize spot" (any place you designate to gather them together again) to unwrap it.

HELPFUL HINT:

- Some suggestions for pictures are the TV set, bookshelf, VCR, VHS tapes, sofa, armchair, stove, refrigerator, microwave, bathtub, toilet, bedroom furniture, curtains, toys—in fact, just about anywhere safe and accessible that you can find pictured in a magazine!

TREASURE HUNT

THE GAME: Children work together in groups of 2 to decipher a treasure map and find the hidden "X," which they exchange for treasure.

AGE LEVEL: 4–10

NUMBER OF PLAYERS: 2–12

APPROXIMATE PREPARATION TIME: 30 minutes

ESTIMATED TIME FOR GAME: 15 minutes

MATERIALS NEEDED:

- treasure maps—1 for every 2 children (see instructions for making the maps below)
- 3" (7.5 cm) square slips of paper marked "X"—same number as treasure maps
- treasure chest—any small, old chest—or improvise by decorating a small cardboard box or shoe box
- treasure—enough to divide equally among all the party guests (see suggestions below)

SUGGESTIONS FOR TREASURE: Any or all of the following: candy necklaces, bracelets, and watches; pennies; colored candy for gems; gummie worms (you can tell the children that the treasure is so old that worms got into it); plastic jewelry, small toys and trinkets—keeping in mind the age of the guests.

BEFORE THE PARTY: Fill the chest with "treasure." You may wish to divide the treasure into individual sandwich bags within the treasure chest for convenience. However, this is a trade-off, because while the booty is easier to divide using sandwich bags, it looks less treasure-like. Next, hide the slips of paper marked "X," indoors or out, making sure no two are very close together. After hiding each slip of paper, make a treasure map, working backwards from the hidden slip of paper to a starting point of your choice.

To make the maps, take child-size steps and for each step you take, make one footprint (or other mark) on the map. Change directions often, but go only straight east, west, north, or south to avoid mistakes a child might make in angle degree. For younger children use large objects around the yard or room as landmarks on the map. For older children avoid landmarks, especially near the end of the map, to prevent the players from just looking towards the end of the map and skipping all the steps involved in finding the paper marked "X." *Important:* After your maps are finished, test them by doing a trial run to make sure everything is marked correctly.

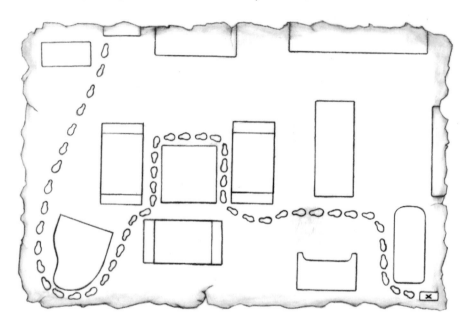

HOW TO PLAY: The object of the game is to find the hidden paper marked "X," which will be exchanged for the treasure. Give each group of two children a map and explain how to read it. For older children you may want to make up a clue in the form of a simple riddle to help them find the starting point of their map. For younger children, you can just show them the starting point. Then sit back and let the children work their way through the map. If they need help, give it to them.

HELPFUL HINTS:
- Children love this type of activity—simple clues with a treasure to reward their efforts.
- The treasure hunt can be as simple or elaborate as your energy and imagination dictate.

PUZZLING PUZZLES

• • • • • • • • • • • • • • • • • • •

THE GAME: Children work together to find all the pieces of a puzzle, assemble the puzzle, and then solve the written or picture riddle on the back of the puzzle, which in turn will lead them to their prizes.

AGE LEVEL: 4–12

NUMBER OF PLAYERS: 1–up (see chart below)

APPROXIMATE PREPARATION TIME: 5 minutes or longer, depending on the size of the puzzle you are using

ESTIMATED TIME FOR GAME: 10–20 minutes, depending on the size of the puzzle

MATERIALS NEEDED:
- 1 puzzle (number of pieces depends on the age of children at party—see chart below)
- 2 pieces of cardboard, each big enough to assemble the puzzle on (if the puzzle is the type that you assemble in a tray as opposed to one that comes in a box, only one piece of cardboard is needed)
- masking tape or cellophane tape
- ink pen or marker
- paper cups—1 per guest—large enough to hold 1 or more puzzle pieces
- prizes—1 per party guest

BEFORE THE PARTY: To determine the size of the puzzle you will need, see the following chart:

Average Age of Children	Size of Puzzle	Maximum Number of Players
4 years	12–15 pieces	5
5–6 years	15–30 pieces	10
6–8 years	25–65 pieces	15
8–12 years	50–100 pieces	20

Average the ages of the children who will be attending, because older children can always help younger children, if they need to. After determining the size of the puzzle needed, assemble the puzzle in its tray or on a piece of cardboard big enough to hold the whole puzzle. Cover the puzzle with another piece of cardboard the same size as the first. Holding the two pieces of cardboard tightly together, flip the puzzle over. You may need to tape the edges of the cardboard together before flipping the puzzle to keep the puzzle from sliding out. On the back side of the puzzle draw a picture for prereaders or write a riddle for older children telling where they can find their prizes.

Some sample pictures are: 1) a picture of a bed (the prizes would then be hidden on a bed somewhere in the house), 2) a picture of the refrigerator (the prizes would then be hidden in the refrigerator), and 3) a picture of a couch (the prizes would be hidden under couch cushions).

Some sample riddles are: 1) I'm long and narrow and people snuggle up on me at night (the prizes would be hidden on a bed), 2) Every day someone opens my mouth and stuffs me with letters (the prizes would be in the mailbox), and 3) Boy, I sure hope no one wants to get clean today, because if they do, not only will I get stepped on but I'll also get all wet (the prizes would be hidden in a shower or bathtub). The older the children, the more challenging the riddles should be.

After drawing a picture or writing a riddle on the back of the puzzle, disassemble the puzzle and hide the pieces around the party room. Be sure to count the exact number of pieces before hiding them, because some puzzles round off the number of pieces to the nearest 5. When hiding the puzzle pieces, keep the ages of the children in mind: the younger the children, the easier the pieces should be to find. None of the pieces should be too hard to find or the game will take too long to play.

Next, wrap the prizes and put them in the place shown on the back of the puzzle.

HOW TO PLAY: Give each child a paper cup. Explain to the children that there are puzzle pieces hidden around the room and that they will need to find them and put them in their cups. If the puzzle you are using has a small number of pieces, tell the children the maximum number of pieces each one is allowed to find to ensure that everyone finds at least one. If there are any pieces still hidden after all the children find at least one, then they can keep looking. Once all of the puzzle pieces have been found, the children should work together to assemble the puzzle. The puzzle needs to be assembled either in the tray it came with, or on the piece of cardboard you used to assemble the puzzle earlier.

After the children finish putting the puzzle together, flip it over, and the children will find the picture or riddle clue on the back. Once they decipher it, they will discover where their prizes are hidden.

HELPFUL HINT:
- If you have a large group of younger children, you may wish to use more than one puzzle so that everyone can find more than one puzzle piece. If you do this, hide the puzzle pieces in different areas of the room, keeping all the pieces to each puzzle in one area. Also, use a different picture on the back of each puzzle so that the prizes are in different locations.

POP-A-PRIZE

THE GAME: Children search through a pile of blown-up balloons, popping them as they go, looking for a slip of paper with a prize number on it.

AGE LEVEL: Version 1—5–12; version 2—3–5

NUMBER OF PLAYERS: 1–10

APPROXIMATE PREPARATION TIME: 25 minutes

ESTIMATED TIME FOR GAME: 10 minutes

MATERIALS NEEDED:
- balloons—at least 3 per guest
- small slips of paper—1 for each balloon
- prizes—1 per guest (the prizes should not all be the same)

BEFORE THE PARTY: Wrap the prizes and number them, starting with number 1 and continuing through to the last prize. Number some of the small slips of paper so each slip matches one prize number. Leave the rest of the slips blank. Fold the slips and tuck them inside the balloons. Blow up all the balloons and contain them in a large plastic leaf bag or in pillowcases.

HOW TO PLAY: The object of the game is to win a prize by finding a balloon with a prize number inside.

Version 1: Have the children stand in a circle. Dump the bag (or bags) of blown-up balloons (the more you have, the more fun the game) into the middle of the circle. Tell the children they need to stomp on the balloons in order to pop them, and then check the paper inside to see if it has a prize number. The children can continue stomping on balloons until everyone finds a numbered slip of paper (most of the slips won't have numbers on them). When everyone has a numbered slip, the children get to exchange the slip for the prize that matches their number. This is a very rambunctious game and is best played by children who are five years old and older.

Version 2: If you have younger children in attendance, you can tone down the game to accommodate them. Have the children stand in a circle. Dump the balloons in the middle. Have each child pick one balloon and go back to his place. Next, have the children pop their balloons one at a time, checking the slip of paper to see if it has a number on it. Have the children who do not get numbered slips continue to pick balloons and pop them one at a time until everyone has a numbered slip. Exchange slips for prizes. For this version, it is better not to have as many balloons because it takes longer to play.

HELPFUL HINTS:
- You might have to help some of the younger party guests pop their balloons.
- Be sure all balloon pieces are picked up immediately if pets or younger children are in attendance, so the pieces don't wind up in anyone's mouth.

DR. KNOTS
• • • • • • • • • • •

THE GAME: Children "knot" themselves up with each other while holding hands; then "Dr. Knots" comes and figures out how to untangle everyone.

AGE LEVEL: 5–12

NUMBER OF PLAYERS: 5–20

APPROXIMATE PREPARATION TIME: None

ESTIMATED TIME FOR GAME: 10 minutes per round

MATERIALS NEEDED:
- large open space
- prizes (optional)

BEFORE THE PARTY: Check the area in which the game will be played to make sure that there are no sharp objects or furniture on which a child might fall and get hurt.

HOW TO PLAY: Choose one player to be Dr. Knots. Have that player leave the room or play area. Next, have the remaining children hold hands and form a circle. Explain to the children that they need to knot themselves up in any way they wish *without* anyone letting go of anyone else's hand. To do this, the children can step under or over each other's arms; they can crawl between each other's legs; and they can twist around to get all tangled up; *but they cannot let go of each other's hands!*

When they consider themselves to be sufficiently tangled, tell the children that they need to call for Dr. Knots by yelling **"HELP! DR. KNOTS! WE NEED YOU!"** At this point the child who was picked to be Dr. Knots can return to the room or play area. He or she will then need to assess the tangled, knotted children and try to untangle them without having anyone let go of anyone else's hand. If Dr. Knots cannot untangle the mess of children, the players in the circle can give hints about how they managed to get into such a tangle. When Dr. Knots has everyone untangled, the round is over. A new Dr. Knots is picked before starting the next round, and play continues in this manner until everyone who wants to be Dr. Knots has had a turn.

There may not always be a successful ending to each round, because quite often the kids end up in such a tangled mess that they just cannot hold hands any longer without falling down. If this happens, be sure to set the tone of laughter and fun, not failure, and then either have the same child be Dr. Knots again so that he/she gets another chance or just move on to the next player, giving someone else a chance to be Dr. Knots.

HELPFUL HINTS:

- Have a designated area already picked out for Dr. Knots to go to. It might be nice to have a table and chair in the area for the good Doctor to use while waiting to be called. On the table you could place several kids' books and magazines, as well as some paper, crayons, and markers. This will help the waiting time pass faster.
- If you plan to give out prizes after this game, toy doctor's equipment such as plastic stethoscopes, thermometers, rubber gloves, and small packs of Band-Aids go well with the theme of the game.

RIDDLE HUNT
• • • • • • • • • • • • • •

THE GAME: Children work either individually or in groups of two to decipher riddles that will eventually lead to their prize.

AGE LEVEL: 6–12 (children need to be able to read to play this game)

NUMBER OF PLAYERS: 1–16 (working in groups of 2)

APPROXIMATE PREPARATION TIME: About 20 minutes per set of riddles

ESTIMATED TIME FOR GAME: 15 minutes

MATERIALS NEEDED:
- slips of paper—5 per child or per group of 2 children
- cellophane tape
- pen
- prizes—1 per child

BEFORE THE PARTY: To set up this game you must first come up with four different riddles per child or group, with no two children or groups having any of the same riddles.

Some sample riddles and their answers are:
> When I'm on I'm very noisy; when I'm off I'm oh so quiet. All kids like to watch me, 'cause my shows are such a riot. (*television*)
>
> I have four legs but I cannot walk, I have a head but I cannot talk. I hold the food when it's time to eat, but I have no hands and no real feet. (*table*)
>
> I'm so flat and lazy, I lie around on the floor all day. I get stepped on and walked on but I never get to play. (*rug*)
>
> I'm comfy and soft. I will keep your head feeling good while you sleep. (*pillow*)
>
> Brrr . . . . . It sure is cold in here. These ice cubes freeze me up! (*freezer*)

Some things that you might want to write riddles about: chair; couch; phone; bookshelf (or even a specific book that would be familiar to kids); TV; VCR; specific video cassettes familiar to kids; computer; refrigerator; stove; sink; table; dishwasher; microwave;

light switch; toilet; bathtub; towels; bed; dresser; curtains; door; specific toys; and anything else kids will recognize. Write one riddle on each of the first four slips of paper for each group, making sure to scatter the riddles for each group around different parts of the house, so that everyone is not in the same room at the same time.

On the fifth slip for each group write the words "YOU FOUND IT" or something similar. Number the riddles in each group 1–4, put the number 5 on the fifth slip, and tape it to the prize or prizes for the group.

Next, you need to hide the riddles. Take the first group of riddles and read riddle #1, then set it aside to give to group 1 as their starting riddle. Hide riddle #2 somewhere on the object depicted in riddle #1. For example, my first sample riddle depicts a television set, so I would hide riddle #2 somewhere on the television set. Before hiding riddle #2, read it so that you will know where to hide riddle #3. My second riddle depicts a table, so I would hide riddle #3 somewhere on the table (probably taped underneath). Hide riddle #4 somewhere on the object depicted in riddle #3, and hide the prizes somewhere on the object depicted in riddle #4. Repeat these steps for all of the sets of riddles.

HOW TO PLAY: The object of this game is to decipher a riddle that will lead to other riddles, which will eventually lead to a prize. Each child or group of children is given their own starting riddle. They must decipher the riddle to figure out where to find their next riddle, which in turn must be deciphered to find another riddle and eventually their prize.

HELPFUL HINT:
- This game is a little harder and much more time-consuming to set up than the other games in this book, but children really enjoy the challenge of playing it. In fact, it is my seven-year-old daughter's favorite in the whole book.

FOAMY FUN

THE GAME: Children have fun spraying each other with shaving cream until their cans are empty; then they rinse off in a sprinkler.

AGE LEVEL: 6–12

NUMBER OF PLAYERS: 2–12

APPROXIMATE PREPARATION TIME: 5 minutes

ESTIMATED TIME FOR GAME: 20 minutes

MATERIALS NEEDED:
- cans of shaving cream—1 per child
- towels—1 per child
- plastic grocery bags—1 per child
- hose and sprinkler

BEFORE THE PARTY: This is a summer game that needs to be played outside. When making the invitations for the party, indicate that guests should wear bathing suits under their clothes, bring a change of clothes, or bring their bathing suit to the party to change into. The playing area for this game will be your yard, so be sure to check it carefully to make sure there are no toys or dangerous objects lying around that could cause a child to fall and get hurt. Hook up the hose and sprinkler and place them out of the way against the wall of the house. Gather enough towels so that each child will have one. These are for drying off, and can be brought by the children; just indicate on the invitations that each child needs to bring a towel.

HOW TO PLAY: Before playing this game, give everyone a plastic grocery bag for their belongings and then have them don their swimsuits. Have everyone gather around so that you can explain the rules of the game. The rules are: 1) No spraying shaving cream in anyone else's face. 2) No ganging up against one person. 3) No pushing or shoving. 4) If someone seriously asks you to please stop spraying them, stop. 5) When all cans are empty, turn on the sprinkler and have fun rinsing off. 6) No coming into the house until all shaving cream has been rinsed off. Add any additional rules of your own. When everyone understands the rules, give each child a can of shaving cream and get out of the way!

HELPFUL HINTS:
- It is best to buy sensitive skin shaving cream.
- It is a good idea to play this game last, so that kids do not have to get into dry clothes again to finish the party.
- Place a couple of small hand towels in a convenient spot for the kids to use to wipe off any shaving cream that accidentally gets on their faces. Let the children know where these are and what they are for when explaining the rules.

ANIMAL ANTICS
• • • • • • • • • • • • • • • • • •

THE GAME: Children try to discover the name of, and then act like, the animal taped on their partner's back, while trying to keep their partner from discovering the animal name taped on their own back.

AGE LEVEL: 6–12 (children need to be able to read to play this game)

NUMBER OF PLAYERS: 2–16

APPROXIMATE PREPARATION TIME: 10 minutes

ESTIMATED TIME FOR GAME: 10 minutes

MATERIALS NEEDED:
- 4" (10 cm) square slips of paper—1 per guest
- tape
- black or dark marker
- prizes (optional)—1 per guest

BEFORE THE PARTY: Write the name of a different animal on each piece of 4" (10 cm) square paper using a black or dark-colored marker. Write the letters as big as each piece of paper will allow.

HOW TO PLAY: The object of the game is to try to see the name of the animal on another child's back and act like that animal while trying to keep that child from seeing the animal on your back. Begin by having all the children stand in a line side by side. Being careful not to let any of the children see the animal names, tape one to each child's back. Next, pair the children off in groups of two (or three if there is an odd number of children) according to where they are standing (the first two children form the first group, the next two become the next group, etc.).

Before play begins, explain the rules: 1) You are not allowed to touch your partner. 2) You cannot tell children in other groups what animals are on the backs of their partners. 3) Once you discover what your partner's animal is, you must act like that animal in every way you can think of. The game is over when all the children have discovered their partners' animals and are acting like those animals. If you are using the option of prizes, they can be passed out after the game is over.

HELPFUL HINTS:
- Before this game is played, check your playing area for any objects that might cause injury and move them out of the way. This game, by its very nature, tends to be very rambunctious and loud.
- If you have younger guests who cannot read but would really like to play this game, pictures of animals can be used instead of words. Just be sure to partner smaller children with other children of about the same size.

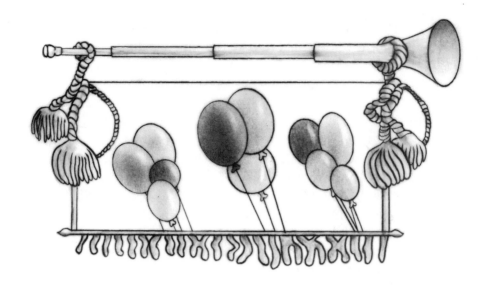

ACTIVITIES

Games are fun, but not everyone wants to spend all their party time playing them. Also, sometimes your party group may be too small to lend itself well to games. This next section focuses on fun party activities. The majority of these activities are best done with no more than six or eight children; however, some can be done with larger groups, especially if you have one or more helpers. All can be done with one child alone.

Many have an end product that the children will be making to take home with them. I recommend that, for those activities, you allow some time before the party to make a sample—not necessarily to show to the children, although that's sometimes helpful, but rather so that you will understand and be familiar with the steps involved in the process. It's a lot easier to work through any confusion beforehand than while trying to explain things to a group of impatient little guests.

WONDERFUL WATER PLAY

THE ACTIVITY: The children play with various items to see if they sink or float and to have fun pouring, dumping, and filling some of the items with water.

AGE LEVEL: 2–6

NUMBER OF PLAYERS: 1–9 unless there are more adults

APPROXIMATE PREPARATION TIME: 5 to 10 minutes

ESTIMATED TIME FOR ACTIVITY: 20 minutes

MATERIALS NEEDED:
- dishpan-sized tubs—1 per every 3 children
- a variety of toys that can be used in water (see suggestions below)
- folding chairs that can get wet—1 per tub
- large towels (if doing the water play indoors)—1 per chair
- waterproof smocks—1 per child (see directions for making waterproof smocks on page 98)
- masking tape or other tape

BEFORE THE PARTY: Gather together a wide variety of toys and plastic dishes that can be used in water. If you need them, make waterproof smocks. Set out the folding chairs around the yard or room, leaving a couple of feet between them. If doing this activity indoors, place a large towel under each chair to help absorb water spills. Place a dishpan tub on each chair and then divide the water toys among the tubs.

WHAT TO DO: Have each child don a waterproof smock. Separate the children into groups of three and have each group stand by a chair, one child on each of the three front sides. Fill the tubs with water, then let the children have fun pouring water from one container to another and experimenting with objects that sink and float.

SUGGESTIONS FOR TOYS TO USE: Plastic eggs; toy cars; small stones; marbles; plastic spoons; metal spoons; plastic barrettes; small building blocks; sieves; cups; bowls; and sponges.

- Chairs are recommended because of their height in relation to kids. However, other surfaces of the same height will work just as well, and if there is no back to the surface, four kids can share a tub of water.

SHAVING CREAM FUN
• •

THE ACTIVITY: Children have fun finger-painting with plain or colored shaving cream.

AGE LEVEL: 2–8

NUMBER OF PLAYERS: 1–unlimited, depending on space

APPROXIMATE PREPARATION TIME: Less than 5 minutes

ESTIMATED TIME FOR ACTIVITY: 20 minutes

MATERIALS NEEDED:
- 1 can of shaving cream
- large flat surface such as a tabletop
- plastic disposable tablecloth
- popsicle sticks—at least 1 per child
- cookie cutters in basic shapes—at least 1 per child
- a helper to clean up after the activity while the party continues
- freezer paper (optional)—one or two rolls (for lifting any designs that the kids wish to save)
- food coloring (optional)
- paint smocks (optional)—1 for each child

BEFORE THE PARTY: Gather together the popsicle sticks and the cookie cutters. If you plan to use food coloring, you will need to have 1 paint smock per child. Old T-shirts work well or you can make your own smocks according to the directions on page 98. If you are planning to lift the kids' designs, cut the white freezer paper to your desired size: 16" (40 cm) square is a good working size. Cut at least 1 sheet per child, but be prepared for the kids to want to make several pictures each. Cover the table with the plastic disposable tablecloth.

WHAT TO DO: Have the children sit or stand around the table or whatever flat surface you are using. If you are adding food coloring to the shaving cream, give each child a paint smock to wear. You can use paint smocks even when you're not using food coloring, but you don't need to, because shaving cream is just soap and will easily wipe off the kids' clothes with a dry or slightly dampened cloth.

When everyone is ready, squirt a large pile of shaving cream in front of each child. If you are using food coloring, add a few drops to each child's pile. The children can then use their hands to spread, squish, and draw in the shaving cream.

While they are playing in the shaving cream, pass out the popsicle sticks and cookie cutters. If you plan to lift any of the children's designs, tell them to let you know when they draw a picture that they really wish to keep.

To lift a picture, gently place a piece of white freezer paper on top of the picture, then carefully rub over the entire back of the paper, pressing down firmly. This will transfer or lift a copy of the picture from the table to the paper. Slowly lift the paper off and place it in an out-of-the-way area until dry. You can rig up a temporary clothesline for hanging pictures to dry by stretching a length of yarn across one end of the room or outside. You can hang the pictures by using spring-type clothespins.

When everyone is finished, or after a set period of time, have the children wash their hands and, using a dry or slightly dampened cloth, wipe off any shaving cream from their clothes. Clean up the play area using a wet dishcloth, being sure to keep it well rinsed while cleaning up.

HELPFUL HINTS:

- Children really enjoy it if you draw a simple picture such as a smiley face with the shaving cream instead of just squirting out a blob in front of them.
- Don't forget to write the children's names on the freezer paper before placing the paper on the pictures to be lifted.

PLAYDOUGH FUN
· ·

THE ACTIVITY: Children have fun playing with Playdough.

AGE LEVEL: 2–8

NUMBER OF PLAYERS: 1–unlimited, depending on space

APPROXIMATE PREPARATION TIME: 5 minutes unless you need to make your own dough (see page 114)

ESTIMATED TIME FOR ACTIVITY: 15 minutes

MATERIALS NEEDED:
- Playdough—1 good-sized ball per child
- ice-cream sticks—1 per child
- miscellaneous gadgets (forks, spoons, small containers, small plates, cookie cutters, etc.)
- plastic or vinyl place mats—1 per child

BEFORE THE PARTY: Put the gadgets you'll be giving the kids with the place mats, ice-cream sticks (used for cutting Playdough), and Playdough. If you need to make your own dough, you'll find a recipe on page 114.

WHAT TO DO: Have the children gather around a table and give one place mat to each child. Explain that you would like them to try to keep their Playdough on their place mats; this makes cleanup much easier. Next, give each child a ball of Playdough and an ice-cream stick to use. Place the rest of the gadgets in the center of the table for everyone to use as needed.

HELPFUL HINTS:
- While the children are playing, use some extra Playdough to show them how to make different things, such as: a) snakes, bracelets, and necklaces by rolling the Playdough, b) how to flatten the Playdough so that they can use the cookie cutters, c) how to make Playdough "food" to put on the small plates, d) how to use the ice-cream stick as a "knife" to cut the Playdough.
- After this activity is finished, the Playdough makes a nice gift for each child to take home. Just place it in a plastic zip-top sandwich bag with the child's name written on it.

SPRINKLER FUN

THE ACTIVITY: In this simple but time-honored activity, children have fun getting wet and burning up excess energy while playing in the sprinklers.

AGE LEVEL: 2–10

NUMBER OF PLAYERS: 1–6 per sprinkler

APPROXIMATE PREPARATION TIME: 5 minutes

ESTIMATED TIME FOR ACTIVITY: 20 minutes

MATERIALS NEEDED:
- 1 or 2 sprinklers
- 1 or 2 outdoor water hoses
- 1 or 2 outdoor faucets
- towels—1 per child
- plastic grocery bags—1 per child
- (optional) squirt guns; cups; bowls and other toys that can be used to hold and throw water; large buckets to hold toys

BEFORE THE PARTY: Place a towel for each child in an area near the sprinkler, but where the towels will not get wet. Gather the water toys, if you wish to use them, and place them in large buckets around the sprinkler area. Hook up the hose to the outdoor faucet. Attach the sprinkler to the other end of the hose. Place the sprinkler in the area that will be used for play. If you are using two sprinklers, try to place them so that their spray overlaps only a little, leaving some gaps of dry spots for kids to run to. Test the spray area by turning the sprinkler(s) on.

Be sure to let the parents of the children know that sprinkler play will be an event at your child's party. Ask the parents to send their kids with their swimsuits already on under their clothes, or at the very least to send the swimsuits in a plastic bag.

Decide on any rules that you would like to set up, such as: 1) No pushing. 2) No throwing water in anyone's face. 3) No grabbing toys from anyone else, etc.

WHAT TO DO: When the time comes for this activity, have the children put on—or strip down to—their swimsuits. Give each child a plastic grocery bag for clothes and possessions so that nothing gets mixed up or lost. Make sure the kids use the bags as they remove their clothes. Then have all of the kids sit in a circle in the yard and explain the rules you've decided on. When everyone understands, let the fun begin.

HELPFUL HINTS:
- Write a reminder on the invitations that everyone is to bring or wear swimsuits. When parents call to RSVP, explain why the swimsuits are needed and remind them again.
- It is best to save this activity for the very last event of the party. That way, the children only have to change once, and they can play until their parents arrive.

BUBBLE BLOWING FUN

THE ACTIVITY: Children have fun blowing and making bubbles using a variety of objects.

AGE LEVEL: 3–8

NUMBER OF PLAYERS: 1–12 per adult

APPROXIMATE PREPARATION TIME: 10 minutes

ESTIMATED TIME FOR ACTIVITY: 15 minutes

MATERIALS NEEDED:
- small dishpans or similar containers—1 for every 4 children
- homemade bubble solution—1 mixture per container
- dish soap—½ cup per mixture
- water—just under 2 cups per mixture
- sugar—3 teaspoons per mixture
- miscellaneous gadgets—several per container (see suggestions below)
- good weather—this is an outdoor activity.

SUGGESTIONS FOR GADGETS: plastic straws; spoons with holes in them; pipe cleaners formed into circles; the top four inches (10 cm) of plastic soda bottles of any size; plastic fruit containers; and any other objects that have holes in them

BEFORE THE PARTY: Make 1 mixture of bubble solution in each container by combining the dish soap, water, and sugar right in the containers. Next, divide the gadgets equally among the containers. You may wish to make a large loop—one for each container—by stringing four straws onto a piece of yarn and then tying the ends of the yarn together. These loops can be used to make larger bubbles by pulling them through the air after dipping them in the bubble solution.

WHAT TO DO: Place the containers of bubble solution around the yard with several feet between each one. Divide the children into groups of four or fewer around each container. Show them how to use the various gadgets to make bubbles—some will require blowing and others will need to be pulled through the air. Then let the kids experiment with the various gadgets, blowing and making as many big and small bubbles as they wish.

  • The bubble solution may make the ground around the containers slippery as it gets sloshed or spilled. Remind the children to be careful as they move around making bubbles.

CLOWN WIGS AND FEET

THE ACTIVITY: Children will have fun making, and then wearing, clown wigs and feet.

AGE LEVEL: 3–8

NUMBER OF PLAYERS: 1–8

APPROXIMATE PREPARATION TIME: 20 minutes

ESTIMATED TIME FOR ACTIVITY: 15 minutes

MATERIALS NEEDED:
  • a pattern for clown feet (see page 134 or make your own)
  • small cardboard bowls—16 oz (450 ml) size (available in superstores)—1 per child
  • lightweight cardboard—approximately 8½″ × 11″ (22 × 28 cm)—2 per child + 1 more
  • colored paper, various colors—about 2 sheets per child
  • a hole puncher or other object that can be used to make holes
  • 12″ (30 cm) lengths of yarn—2 per child
  • 6″ (15 cm) lengths of yarn—4 per child
  • crayons or markers
  • clean medicine dosage cups—1 per child
  • cotton swabs—1 per child
  • bottle of glue (washable is best)
  • roll of cellophane tape

BEFORE THE PARTY: Using the extra piece of cardboard, make a larger clown foot pattern from the pattern on page 134. Trace two feet for each child onto the remaining cardboard, and cut them out. Using a hole puncher or other object, punch two holes in each foot in the places indicated on the pattern. Tie the end of the six-inch (15 cm) piece of yarn through each hole. Set the feet aside.

To prepare the clown wigs, punch two holes in each paper bowl, about a half inch from the edge on opposite sides of the bowl. In each hole, tie one of the 12-inch (30 cm) yarn lengths. Next, cut your colored paper into ½-inch strips. When cutting the strips, you can cut either across or down the paper, depending on the length you want the clown hair to be. After cutting all the paper, curl the strips gently, using the edge of a pair of scissors or a similar object, as you would do when curling ribbon for gifts. Place all the curled strips into a bag or other container until ready for use. These curled paper strips will be glued to the outside bottom of the bowls by the children so that the bowls can be worn on the head like a wig with the "clown hair" sticking up all around.

WHAT TO DO: Have the children gather around the work surface and explain that they will be making clown feet and wigs to wear. If you made practice samples, you may want to show them to the children. Pass out the clown feet first and let the children color them in any way they wish, using the crayons and markers.

While the children color their clown feet, prepare the materials for the clown wigs. First, place about ½ inch of glue in each clean medicine cup along with one cotton swab. Next, place all of the curled paper strips in the center of the work table. As the children finish coloring their clown feet, pass out the paper bowls and the glue cups. Show them how to use the cotton swab to place glue on the end of a curled strip of paper and then stick it onto the outside bottom of their bowl. Let the children glue as much clown hair on their bowls as they desire (or as much as time and number of paper strips allows).

When they are finished, they can wear their clown feet and wigs by simply tying them on. Tie one clown foot around each ankle, placing a small piece of curled tape on the toe of each shoe to hold the clown foot on. Tie the clown wig under the chin, with the bowl resting on the crown of the head.

HELPFUL HINTS:

- Be sure to use cardboard bowls. Styrofoam or plastic won't work.
- Before tracing the clown foot pattern onto the lightweight cardboard, punch out the holes in the pattern. Then you can trace where to punch the holes onto the cardboard as well.
- Hole reinforcers can be used to keep the holes on the clown's foot from tearing.
- To achieve the best curl when making the paper strips, use colored paper such as unlined note paper or computer paper. Strips of tracking holes from the edges of colored and white computer paper also work well. You can use construction paper, but it is harder to curl because it tears easily. Also, construction paper does not hold a curl as well as notepaper or computer paper. You can also use curling ribbon, but the glue will not hold it very well, so keep this in mind.
- This activity goes well with face painting (see pages 95–96).
- Don't forget to put the children's names on both of their clown feet as well as their wigs.

PAPER CUP PHONES

THE ACTIVITY: Children decorate two paper cups and then connect them with sturdy string to make their own "telephones."

AGE LEVEL: 3–8

NUMBER OF PLAYERS: 1–8

APPROXIMATE PREPARATION TIME: 10 minutes

ESTIMATED TIME FOR ACTIVITY: 10 minutes

MATERIALS NEEDED:
- 6–8 oz. (180–240 ml) solid-colored paper cups—2 per child
- markers or crayons
- sturdy string—36″ (90 cm) or more per child
- small, flat buttons—2 per child
- 1 sharp pencil

BEFORE THE PARTY: Poke a small hole in the bottom center of each cup with the tip of the sharp pencil. Next, cut your string into 36-inch (90 cm) or longer lengths—1 per child—and tie a small button on one end of each string.

WHAT TO DO: Give each child two paper cups to decorate with the markers and crayons. As the children finish decorating their cups, give them each a string with the button tied to it. Have them thread the string through the hole from the inside to the outside of one cup and then from the outside to the inside of the second cup. When this step is finished, give each child the second button to tie onto the end of the string that they threaded through the holes. Each cup will now have a button inside it.

To use the phones, the children work with partners. Each child holds one cup and then walks away from the other until the string is taut between them. Then they take turns talking and listening into the cups.

HELPFUL HINTS:
- Make sure that the cups you use for these phones are not wax coated, because those are hard to color.
- You can find solid-colored hot/cold cups without wax in most party supply and grocery stores.

TAMBOURINES
• • • • • • • • • • • • • • •

THE ACTIVITY: Kids enjoy listening to music, and they especially like making their own music. These "tambourines" are the perfect way for them to do just that.

AGE LEVEL: 3–8

NUMBER OF PLAYERS: 1–6

APPROXIMATE PREPARATION TIME: 10 minutes

ESTIMATED TIME FOR ACTIVITY: 10 minutes

MATERIALS NEEDED:
- paper plates—1 per child
- markers or crayons
- popcorn seeds—1 handful per child
- tissue paper—various colors
- hot glue gun—cool melt or regular

BEFORE THE PARTY: The only thing that needs to be prepared in advance for this activity is the tissue paper. Cut it into strips that are approximately 1″ × 12″ (5 × 30 cm). Cut at least four per child, but six is better.

WHAT TO DO: Pass out the paper plates to the children. Spread the crayons or markers in the middle of the work surface so that everyone can reach them. Show the children the bottom side of the plate and explain that it is the side of the plate they need to color. While the children are coloring, plug in the hot glue gun to warm it up. As the children finish coloring, show them how to bend their paper plate in half so that their colored design is on both sides of the outside, being careful not to crease the plate on the bend line. The next step is to put glue on the plate. If you have a cool melt glue gun, kids age six and older should be able to put the glue on with your help and supervision. If, however, your gun is a regular hot glue gun, then you should do all the gluing.

Begin by placing a strip of hot glue along two-thirds of the edge of one side of the bent plate. The remaining third will be glued after popcorn seeds and tissue paper streamers are added. Press the two sides together along the edges until the glue dries sufficiently to hold them. Have the child whose plate is being glued get a handful of popcorn seeds and drop them down inside the plate. (Watch smaller children closely so they don't eat the seeds.) Next, have the child pick four to six of the precut tissue strips to use as streamers. Hot glue the rest of the edge of the plate, but before pressing the two sides together, add the streamers. This may require a few more drops of hot glue to keep the streamers from falling out later. When the glue dries completely, the tambourines are finished.

HELPFUL HINTS:
- Make sure each tambourine has the child's name on it.
- If you have a group of mixed-age kids, where some are old enough to use the cool melt glue gun and others are not, it might be easier for everyone to accept if you do *all* the gluing.

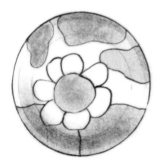

Decorate back of plate.

Fold plate with decorated part on the outside.

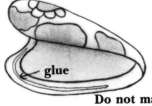

Do not make a sharp crease.

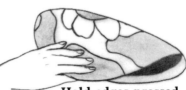

Hold edges pressed together until glue sets.

Add popcorn seeds and streamers.

Finish gluing and hold shut till glue sets.

PAPER PLATE MASKS

THE ACTIVITY: Children make masks using paper plates and a variety of scrap materials.

AGE LEVEL: 3–8

NUMBER OF PLAYERS: 1–8

APPROXIMATE PREPARATION TIME: 15–20 minutes

ESTIMATED TIME FOR ACTIVITY: 20 minutes

MATERIALS NEEDED:
- paper plates—1 per child
- clean medicine dosage cups—1 per child
- cotton swabs—1 per child
- bottle of glue (washable is best)
- safety scissors—1 pair for every 1–2 children
- 12″ (30 cm) lengths of yarn—2 per child
- a variety of scrap materials (see suggestions below)
- hole punch (or a pointed object that can be used to make holes)
- shallow containers (about the size of a cookie sheet or cake pan)—1 for every 3–4 children

SUGGESTIONS FOR SCRAP MATERIALS: markers; crayons; sequins; construction paper; strips of tracking holes from the edges of computer paper; glitter; material scraps; yarn; beads; contact paper; and small plastic gems.

BEFORE THE PARTY: First, cut two eye-holes in each plate, using any shape you desire. The children attending the party can do this step, if you feel they are all capable of doing it. After cutting the eye-holes, use a hole punch or other pointed object and make two small holes on opposite edges of each plate. In each small hole, tie one 12-inch (30 cm) length of yarn. (There should be two pieces of yarn tied to each plate when finished; they will be tied together behind the wearer's head to hold the mask on.)

Next, divide the scrap materials into equal piles and place one pile in each shallow container. Glitter, beads, and sequins can be left in individual containers within the shallow containers.

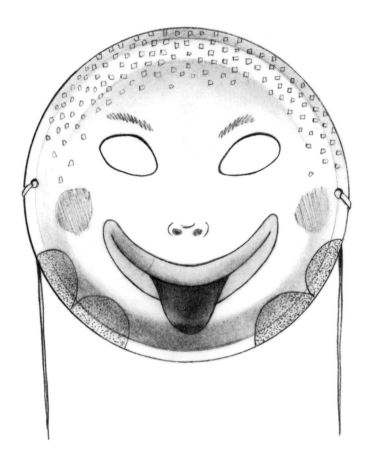

Markers and crayons can be divided equally between the containers or placed in small cups or bowls. Place at least one pair of safety scissors in each container. These containers will be placed around a table so that every three or four children will be sharing one container of materials.

WHAT TO DO: Have the children sit around the table and explain to them that they will be making masks from paper plates. Show the children the materials they'll be using, holding up the various items from one of the containers. Pass out the paper plates that you prepared earlier, one to each child. Place the containers of materials around the table so that every three or four children can share.

While the children are looking through the materials and deciding what to use, squirt about half an inch of glue into each of the medicine cups. Place a cotton swab in each cup and pass one out to each child. This will be the glue supply for making the mask. You can add more glue to each cup as needed.

While the children are making their masks, walk around the table and write their names on their plates. Let the children use their imagination to their hearts' content, and when they are finished, there will be lots of neat masks around the room.

HELPFUL HINTS:

- It's necessary to supervise the use of glitter closely, because children have a tendency to dump a whole bottle onto a small section.
- For younger children, it might be best to keep the glitter yourself and let them know that you will be glad to sprinkle it on their masks if they want some.
- If you do not wish to tie the masks over the children's faces, popsicle sticks can be used to make a handle at the bottom of the masks and the children can just hold the masks in front of their faces. This works well for younger children who do not like to wear masks.
- As the children finish their masks, have them clean up the section where they were working. After everyone is done, have all the children work together on the final cleanup of the table before continuing on to the next game or activity.

JEWELED CROWNS

THE ACTIVITY: Using plastic gems and markers or crayons, children will decorate cardboard crowns to wear.

AGE LEVEL: 3–8

NUMBER OF PLAYERS: 1–8

APPROXIMATE PREPARATION TIME: 15–20 minutes, depending upon the number of crowns

ESTIMATED TIME FOR ACTIVITY: 15 minutes

MATERIALS NEEDED:
- crown pattern (found on page 135, or make one of your own)
- lightweight cardboard—approximately 11″ × 14″ (27.5 × 35 cm)—1 piece per child plus an additional piece for tracing the pattern
- pen or pencil
- glue
- cotton swabs—1 per child
- clean medicine dosage cups—1 per child
- plastic gems with flat backs—several per child
- markers and/or crayons
- cellophane tape

BEFORE THE PARTY: Cut a 2½″ × 14″ (6 × 35 cm) strip off the edge of each piece of cardboard including the extra piece. Set the strips aside; they will be used as the back strips for the crowns. Next, trace the crown pattern from page 135 onto the extra piece, or make your own crown pattern on lightweight cardboard. Cut out the pattern and use it for tracing crowns onto the rest of the lightweight cardboard, making sure you have enough for one crown per child. Cut out all the pieces. Glue or tape one end of each back strip to one end of each front strip for each crown.

WHAT TO DO: Pass out the crowns, one to each child. Place the markers and/or crayons in the center so that all the children can reach them, and let the children color their own crowns. While they are coloring, pour about ¼ inch of glue into each medicine cup, then place one cotton swab in each cup. As the children finish coloring their crowns, give them a medicine cup of glue and a handful of plastic gems to glue onto their crowns.

When they finish gluing the gems onto the crowns, measure the crowns around their heads, taping the other end of the back strip to the front piece so that each crown fits the wearer's head.

HELPFUL HINTS:

- This activity is good to do following the Ancient Treasure Dig game.
- To add variety to the crowns, use more than one pattern.

PAPER BAG PUPPETS

THE ACTIVITY: The children will have fun making and then playing with their very own paper bag puppets.

AGE LEVEL: 3–10

NUMBER OF PLAYERS: 1–8

APPROXIMATE PREPARATION TIME: 10 minutes

ESTIMATED TIME FOR ACTIVITY: 15 minutes

MATERIALS NEEDED:
- lunch bags—1 per child
- markers and/or crayons
- construction paper—various colors (scrap pieces are okay)
- miscellaneous materials such as: self-sticking hole reinforcers, scraps of yarn, strips of tracking holes from the edges of computer paper, buttons, material scraps, and anything else that might be interesting on a puppet
- safety scissors—1 pair for every 1–2 children
- glue
- cotton swabs—1 per child
- clean medicine dosage cups—1 per child

BEFORE THE PARTY: Bring together all the materials you'll be allowing the children to use for making their puppets. If the children are too young to cut shapes easily from the construction paper, precut several circles, squares, and other shapes for them to use for eyes, ears, noses, mouths, etc.

WHAT TO DO: Have the children gather around a table and explain to them that they will be making puppets using paper lunch bags. Pass out the paper bags. Be sure each bag has the child's name on it.

When everyone has a bag, show the children how the puppet will work by placing your hand in a bag, curling your fingers around the fold at the bottom of the bag, and then moving your fingers to make the bag "talk." Show the children where they will need to make their puppets' mouths—at the fold near the bottom of the bag—in order for their puppets to "talk" correctly.

Place the markers, crayons, and the various materials in the center of the table, suggesting possible uses for some of the different things, such as: 1) yarn or strips of tracking holes from computer paper make great hair, 2) hole reinforcers, buttons, or various shapes cut from construction paper make neat-looking eyes and noses, and 3) scraps of material or construction paper are good for making clothes.

While the children look through the materials and make their selections, place one cotton swab and about ¼ inch of glue in each medicine cup and give one to each child. Show the children how to use the cotton swab to put glue on their bags and materials to make their puppets.

Let the children make a puppet any way they wish.

HELPFUL HINT:

- If you make a practice sample to show to the children, make it very simple so that young children are not intimidated by it or upset that they cannot make theirs look like yours.

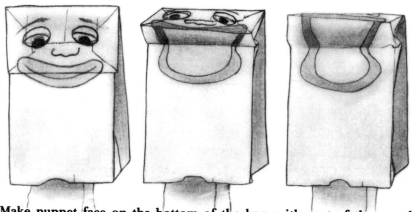

Make puppet face on the bottom of the bag, with part of the mouth below the bottom when the bag is folded.

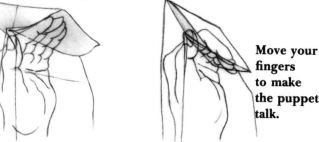

Place your hand in the bag, like this.

Move your fingers to make the puppet talk.

BELL CATCHER
• • • • • • • • • • • • • • • •

THE ACTIVITY: Using a paper cup, a bell, a button, and some yarn, children make a toy that they will have fun playing with.

AGE LEVEL: 3–10

NUMBER OF PLAYERS: 1–8

APPROXIMATE PREPARATION TIME: 10 minutes

ESTIMATED TIME FOR ACTIVITY: 10 minutes

MATERIALS NEEDED:
- 6-oz. hot/cold solid-colored paper cups—1 per child
- medium-sized bells (available from crafts stores, superstores, Christmas stores)—1 per child
- small, flat buttons—1 per child
- 12″ (30 cm) lengths of yarn—1 per child
- markers or crayons
- sharp pencil or other pointed object

BEFORE THE PARTY: Tie a button on one end of each length of yarn. Next, poke a small hole in the bottom of each cup using the sharp pencil or other pointed object.

WHAT TO DO: Pass out the cups to the children, writing their names on them as you do, and have the children color the cups in any way they want. As each child finishes, give him/her a piece of the yarn with the button attached and instructions to stick the yarn down through the hole in the bottom of the cup from inside the cup so that when the yarn is pulled tight, the button is lying on the inside bottom of the cup. As the children finish this step, give them a bell to tie onto the dangling end of the yarn. Some children may need help tying the bell onto the yarn.

To use the bell catcher, hold the cup in your hand and try to swing the bell around and catch it with the cup.

HELPFUL HINTS:
- For younger children it is better to use larger bells. However, older children find medium-sized bells more of a challenge to catch.
- Bell catchers also make nice prizes.

SCRUMPTIOUS FLOWERS
• •

THE ACTIVITY: The children will make scrumptious flowers using gumdrops and cookies on pipe cleaners. This is a great snack that kids enjoy making as much as they do eating.

AGE LEVEL: 3–10

NUMBER OF PLAYERS: 1–8

APPROXIMATE PREPARATION TIME: 5 minutes

ESTIMATED TIME FOR ACTIVITY: 10 minutes

MATERIALS NEEDED:
- 6-oz. (180 ml) cups—1 per child plus 1 extra
- stickers (any pattern)—several per child
- cookies with scalloped edges and a hole in the center—5 per child plus a few extra
- gumdrops—5 per child plus a few extra
- green pipe cleaners—5 per child plus a few extra
- Ping-Pong-sized balls of Playdough—1 per child

BEFORE THE PARTY: Separate the stickers into equal piles, one pile for each child. Next, cut the pipe cleaners to a length of about three inches (7½ cm) above the top of the cups you are using when the pipe cleaners are placed inside one of the cups. Prepare your balls of Playdough and place one in each cup. The balls do not have to be perfectly round or exactly the same size—they will just be used to weigh down the bottoms of the cups.

WHAT TO DO: Begin this activity by giving each child one cup with the Playdough ball inside it and a pile of stickers. Have them press the Playdough down as flat as they can in the bottom of their cups. Then have them decorate the outside of their cup with the stickers.

While the children are decorating their cups, distribute five pipe cleaners and five gumdrops to each child and to yourself (to demonstrate with). When the kids have finished decorating their cups, show them how to place a gumdrop on the end of each pipe cleaner, with the wider end down and the narrower end up. Then push the pipe cleaner about halfway through the gumdrop. Finally, stick the other end of the pipe cleaner down into the Playdough in the cup so that the gumdrop end is up. After all of the children have finished these steps for all their pipe cleaners, show them how to gently set a cookie over the top of each gumdrop so that the gumdrop shows through the hole in the center of the cookie. These scrumptious "flowers" can be eaten right away or saved and taken home.

HELPFUL HINTS:
- Green pipe cleaners can be found at most craft stores; however, if you cannot find green ones, white ones work just as well.
- When buying the gumdrops, be careful not to get spice drops; many children don't like them.
- Be sure to have several extra cookies to replace any that get broken. Many kids push down too hard while placing the cookies over the gumdrops, which causes breakage.
- It's a good idea to have plenty of gumdrops on hand, because many children will ask for their favorite colors.

Press Playdough down flat in cup.

Decorate cup with stickers.

Put gumdrops on the end of the pipe cleaners.

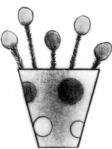

Stick the pipe cleaners in the cup.

Gently set cookies over the gumdrops.

MYSTICAL MAGICAL DOUGH

THE ACTIVITY: Children are fascinated by mystical magical dough, which is made from cornstarch and water. It can be picked up like a solid substance, yet it will melt through the fingers like a thick liquid. One moment it seems to be dry and the next, wet. This activity is really fun.

AGE LEVEL: 3–12

NUMBER OF PLAYERS: 1–unlimited, depending on space

APPROXIMATE PREPARATION TIME: 5 minutes

ESTIMATED TIME FOR ACTIVITY: 15 minutes

MATERIALS NEEDED:
- shallow containers at least ½ inch deep—1 for every 2 children
- cornstarch—1¼ cups per container
- water—⅔ cup per container
- old T-shirts or paint smocks—1 per child

BEFORE THE PARTY: First, gather your containers together. Cookie sheets work well because their sides are high enough to keep the mystical magical dough in the pan but not so high that they hinder play. Next, measure out the cornstarch and place it in each container, spreading it over the bottom. Then add the water to each container. Stir with your fingers until thoroughly mixed.

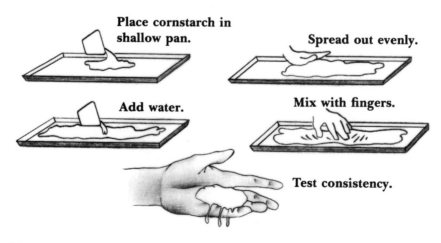

Place cornstarch in shallow pan.

Spread out evenly.

Add water.

Mix with fingers.

Test consistency.

Check the consistency. To do this, first run your fingers through the mixture. There should be some slight resistance. If not, add some more cornstarch, just a teaspoon at a time, until there is some resistance. Next, check to see if you can pick up a handful of the mixture. You should be able to pick up and hold some for just a second, then it should run down through your fingers as though it is melting. If you can't pick up any dough, the mixture is too runny and you need to add more starch. If you can pick up the dough, but it doesn't melt and ooze back down between your fingers, it is too thick and you need to add more water, a few drops at a time. Isn't this fun?

When you have the consistency right, the mystical magical dough is ready. If the children do not play with it within an hour, you will probably need to add a few drops of water to each container. This is because the water tends to evaporate from the mixture rather quickly. If you want to use paint smocks, old T-shirts work well or you can find directions for making home-made paint smocks on page 98.

WHAT TO DO: Divide the children into groups of two or three (two is best) and have them stand around one or more tables. Have everyone put on a paint smock. (This step is optional, because the mystical magical dough is just cornstarch and water and, when dry, can be brushed off clothes easily with a damp cloth. However, paint smocks help to make cleanup a little easier.) Pass out the containers of mystical magical dough, 1 to each group. Let the children have fun just playing in it, swirling their fingers through it, picking some up and watching it melt, etc.

HELPFUL HINTS:
- To minimize any mess the children might make with the dough, you may wish to set some rules, such as: a) Keep your hands and the dough *over the pan* when picking it up. b) No throwing the dough around. c) Do not put the dough in your mouth.
- If you wish to do this activity outside, you can use folding chairs or other easily cleaned chairs instead of a table. Just use one chair per container and have the children stand around it.

TREASURE BOXES
• • • • • • • • • • • • • • • • • •

THE ACTIVITY: From small cardboard boxes children make "treasure boxes" by decorating them with construction paper, markers, buttons, beads, sequins, and any other glitzy or glittery objects you can find.

AGE LEVEL: 3–12

NUMBER OF PLAYERS: 1–8

APPROXIMATE PREPARATION TIME: 15–20 minutes

ESTIMATED TIME FOR ACTIVITY: 15 minutes

MATERIALS NEEDED:
- small cardboard boxes with lids (shoe boxes work well)— 1 per child
- brown construction paper
- markers
- an assortment of buttons, beads, sequins, glitter and anything else you wish to use for decorations on the box
- several small dishes
- glue
- clean medicine dosage cups—1 per child
- cotton swabs—1 per child
- at least one other adult to help

BEFORE THE PARTY: At least a day before the party, cover the four outside edges and the top of the lids of all of the boxes with plain brown construction paper. You can use other colors if desired, but plain brown looks more like wood. By doing this at least a day before the party, the glue has plenty of time to dry. Next, divide your assortment of box decorations equally into several small dishes.

WHAT TO DO: Write the children's names on the boxes and pass them out, explaining that they will be making treasure boxes to take home and keep their special treasures in (as well as their party prizes). Give each child one medicine dosage cup with about ½ inch of glue squeezed into it along with a cotton swab. Place the dishes with the assortment of buttons, beads, sequins, and glitter around the table so that every child can reach at least one dish, and place the markers in the middle of the table. Let the children have fun decorating their boxes.

HELPFUL HINTS:

- If you cannot get any medicine cups for the glue, egg cartons cut into individual little cups work just fine, or you can even use small square pieces of cardboard with the glue squirted in the center.
- Have your adult helper clean up the work area while you play a game in another area with the kids.
- This activity goes well with the Treasure Hunt game on page 47–48. If you decide to do both at your party, make the treasure boxes first. Then the kids can put their "treasure" into their own treasure box when they find it.
- This activity also goes well with the Ancient Treasure Dig game, page 35–36, but you can play the game first. The gems and jewels the kids find can be used to decorate the treasure box as well as to put inside as treasure.

COOKIE DECORATING

THE ACTIVITY: Children decorate sugar cookies with frosting and sprinkles.

AGE LEVEL: 3–12

NUMBER OF PLAYERS: 1–8

APPROXIMATE PREPARATION TIME: 10 minutes

ESTIMATED TIME FOR ACTIVITY: 15 minutes

MATERIALS NEEDED:
- plain shortbread or sugar cookies—2–3 per child
- paper towels and/or washcloths—2 per child
- vanilla frosting—1 tub
- 5 oz. (150 ml) kitchen cups—1 per child
- popsicle sticks—1 per child
- a variety of sprinkles
- several small dishes—at least 1 for each type of sprinkle per every 3–4 children
- paint smocks (optional)—1 per child

BEFORE THE PARTY: Place a scoop of frosting in each cup. Cover the cups with plastic wrap until ready to use. Separate the sprinkles into individual dishes. You will need to have enough small dishes of sprinkles so that every child can reach some sprinkles. If you want to use paint smocks, old T-shirts work well, or you can find directions for homemade paint smocks on page 98.

WHAT TO DO: If you're using paint smocks, have each child don one. If using homemade smocks, tape them across the back. Have the kids gather around the table. Next, wet one paper towel or washcloth per child and have everyone use theirs to wash their hands. When all hands are clean, have the children set their wet paper towels to the side for later use as needed.

Pass out one dry paper towel to each child for use as a "plate," and then give them 3 cookies to place on it. Next, give each child a cup of frosting and one popsicle stick "knife." Have the children begin frosting their cookies. While they're doing it,

88

place the small dishes of sprinkles around the table. As the children finish frosting their cookies, remove the cups of frosting and let them use the sprinkles. When the cookies are decorated, the children can eat them as a snack or save them to take home. If a child wants to save the cookies to take home, write his/her name on the paper towel and then place the cookies in a safe, out-of-the-way location until the party is over.

HELPFUL HINTS:

- Remind the children that they have a wet paper towel to use for wiping their fingers and hands while decorating the cookies. This will, hopefully, keep them from using their clothes or mouths.
- Shortbread cookies are just the suggested cookie. However, you can use any cookie that has a plain top.

NOTABLE NECKLACES

●●●●●●●●●●●●●●●●●●●●●●●●

THE ACTIVITY: These necklaces are made using modelling clay and plaster of Paris in paper cups.

AGE LEVEL: 5–12

NUMBER OF PLAYERS: 1–8

APPROXIMATE PREPARATION TIME: 15 minutes

ESTIMATED TIME FOR ACTIVITY: 10 minutes

MATERIALS NEEDED:
- modelling clay (not Playdough)—1 golf ball–sized lump per child
- 5- or 6-oz. (150–180 ml) paper cups—1 per child
- plaster of Paris compound—1 cup per batch
- water—½ cup per batch
- sharp pencils (1 per child)
- straws—1 per child
- glitter—1 or 2 pinches per child
- thick macramé yarn—18″ (45 cm) lengths—1 per child

BEFORE THE PARTY: One batch of plaster of Paris is enough to make five necklaces. Begin by cutting off the top half of all the paper cups. Then separate the modelling clay into balls and place one ball in each cup. Next, place the plaster of Paris compound in a bowl. Measure the water, but do not add it to the compound; just keep it ready for later. Cut the macramé yarn into 18-inch (45 cm) lengths.

WHAT TO DO: Write each child's name on the bottom of a cup with the modelling clay in it and pass them out. Have the children remove the clay, flatten it on the tabletop, and put it back in the cup, pressing it down. Then, using a sharp pencil, have the children make a design in the clay. The design should not have any deep holes or extra-fine lines.

While the children are making their designs, mix the water into the plaster of Paris compound according to the directions on the compound box. As the children finish their designs, have them push a straw down into the clay near the top of their design but not too close to the edge of the clay. Next, have the children sprinkle a pinch or two of glitter onto their design, if desired. When everyone is finished, pour about half an inch of plaster of Paris onto the clay in each cup. Let it dry for a minimum of 60 minutes while the children do other things.

After at least the minimum drying time has elapsed, carefully tear the paper cup away from the plaster and clay inside and then, just as carefully, remove the clay and the straw from the plaster. Put a piece of macramé yarn through the hole and tie it to complete the necklace. These necklaces need to be handled very carefully until they are completely dry, which takes about 24 hours, so be sure to let the parents know this when they pick up their children after the party.

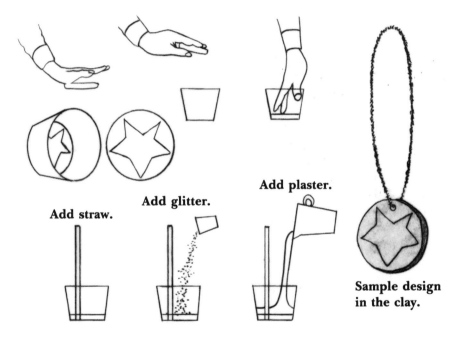

Add straw.

Add glitter.

Add plaster.

Sample design in the clay.

HELPFUL HINTS:

- This activity should be done early in the party to allow for ample drying time.
- If you have a teenage or adult helper, let them remove the paper cups and tie the yarn onto each necklace while you do other things with the party kids.
- Remember to write the children's names on the backs of their necklaces as soon as you remove them from the paper cups, so that no one ends up with the wrong necklace.

PAINT A HAT OR VISOR

THE ACTIVITY: Most children enjoy wearing baseball caps and visors, especially novelty ones. This activity allows kids to decorate a cap or visor in any style they like.

AGE LEVEL: 5–12

NUMBER OF PLAYERS: 1–8

APPROXIMATE PREPARATION TIME: Less than 5 minutes (but add 10 minutes if you want to make homemade paint smocks)

ESTIMATED TIME FOR ACTIVITY: 15 minutes

MATERIALS NEEDED:
- baseball caps or visors—1 per child
- fabric paints—various colors (available at crafts stores and superstores)—minimum of 1 bottle per child
- small beads and/or foil sequins—several per child
- several small containers
- old T-shirts to use as paint smocks or homemade smocks (see page 98)—1 per child
- old newspapers
- 1 piece of scrap cardboard

BEFORE THE PARTY: Gather together all of your materials. Place the beads and/or foil sequins in several small containers. These will be placed around the work surface so that everyone will be able to reach at least one dish.

WHAT TO DO: Give each child a paint smock to wear. While they are putting the paint smocks on, cover the work surface with old newspapers. When everyone is wearing a paint smock, pass out the caps or visors. On a piece of cardboard, show the children how to use the paints to draw pictures, designs, and shapes. Also, show the kids how to stick beads and foil sequins onto the hats by making large dots with the paints. Let the children paint their hats any way they like. When the hats are finished, place them in an out-of-the-way location to dry.

HELPFUL HINTS:
- Because it takes a while for the paints to dry, this activity

should be done at the beginning of the party, and may even be a good starting activity that the kids can begin working on as they arrive.

- Plastic visors are the least expensive type of hat to use for this activity and they work well, especially for younger children, who can easily wipe off the paint if mistakes are made.

PAINT A SHIRT

THE ACTIVITY: Children use shirt paints to paint designs on T-shirts.

AGE LEVEL: 6–12

NUMBER OF PLAYERS: 1–8

APPROXIMATE PREPARATION TIME: 5 minutes (15 if you want homemade paint smocks)

ESTIMATED TIME FOR ACTIVITY: 15 minutes

MATERIALS NEEDED:

- small bottles of fabric paints in a variety of colors—at least 1 bottle per guest
- pieces of sturdy cardboard—8½" × 11" (22 × 28 cm) approximate size—1 per guest
- plain white T-shirts (you may wish to ask the guests to bring their own, but have some extras in case they forget)
- old newspapers to cover the work surface
- paint smocks (old T-shirts or homemade smocks—see page 98)—1 per guest

BEFORE THE PARTY: The only setup involved for this activity is to gather all the materials together.

WHAT TO DO: Have the children put on their paint smocks. While they do it, spread out newspapers to cover the work surface. Pass out the white T-shirts (or have the children get the ones they brought from home). Next, pass out the pieces of cardboard and demonstrate how to place them inside the shirt, explaining as you do so that this will keep the paint from leaking through to the back of the shirt while they are working.

When everyone is ready, place all the shirt paints in the center of the table and let the children begin painting. They can draw pictures with the paint or just do abstract designs. The children may even wish to write sayings on their shirts. As each shirt is finished, put it in an out-of-the-way place to dry.

HELPFUL HINTS:

- It is best to have more than one bottle of paint per child so that no one has to sit around waiting for another color.
- If you cannot get enough cardboard for inside the shirts, folded paper grocery bags will also work.

FACE-PAINTING FUN
• •

THE ACTIVITY: In this fun activity, children take turns painting designs on each other's faces.

AGE LEVEL: 7–12

NUMBER OF PLAYERS: 1–8

APPROXIMATE PREPARATION TIME: Less than 5 minutes

ESTIMATED TIME FOR ACTIVITY: 20 minutes

MATERIALS NEEDED:
- several face paints in a variety of colors (available at super-stores)
- hand towels—1 per every 2 children
- paper—1 sheet per child
- fine-tip markers—at least 1 per child
- 1 or 2 mirrors (or access to a bathroom mirror)
- stickers (optional)—1–3 per child

BEFORE THE PARTY: Gather together all of the materials. The face paints should not all be on one tray, because several children will need to use them at the same time.

WHAT TO DO: Divide the children into groups of two and have them sit around a table. Pass out the paper and markers to the children and tell them to discuss with their partners what they want painted on their face. Then, have each child draw a few practice pictures on their paper using the markers. When they are ready, each group will need to decide who will paint first and who will get their face painted first. The children getting their faces painted first should tuck a hand towel into the front collar of their shirts to keep the paint from getting on their clothes. After the towels are in place, the painting may begin. As the children in each group finish painting their partners' faces, they should change places with each other. When everyone is done, the children can use mirrors to admire each other's artwork.

HELPFUL HINTS:
- If some children absolutely do not want their faces painted,

do not force the issue. Instead, suggest that they have a design painted on the back of their hand or on their arm.

- While the children are painting, remind them not to paint too close to their partner's eyes or mouth.
- It is a good idea to have a jar of cold cream on hand for any children who wish to remove their face paint before leaving the party.
- This is a good activity to do after making clown wigs and shoes.

PARTY PRIZES

Unlike the first two sections of this book, which deal with games and activities involving child participation, this is the "adults only" section. Although some of the projects that follow could be adapted to a child-participation activity, the intent here is to provide you with suggestions and guidelines for making party prizes. Making the prizes is often fun and more satisfying—not to mention less expensive—than buying them; and it gives the environmentally conscious person an opportunity to recycle many throwaways. However, for all you handicraft-challenged individuals out there, there is also included at the end of this section a list of over 100 prizes that can be found in most grocery, discount, or party stores.

HOMEMADE WATERPROOF PAINT SMOCKS
• •

Homemade smocks are not prizes, but they do facilitate the games and activities.

MATERIALS NEEDED:
- small or medium-sized trash bags—1 per smock
- scissors
- masking tape or other tape

PROCEDURE: First, determine the size of the trash bags you will need. For children age six and younger, or for petite children older than six, use small trash bags; for children seven and older, or for huskier younger children, use medium-sized trash bags.

Lay the bag flat on the floor or table and slit it down the center of the front panel. This will become the back opening of the smock. Next, cut the armholes, one on each side of the bag near the bottom seam. The smocks are worn with the seam at the shoulders. Repeat for each smock needed.

The bags are now ready to wear. Put them on the child with the center slit in the back and the bottom seam at the top. Place a piece of tape across the back slit to help keep the smock from sliding off the child.

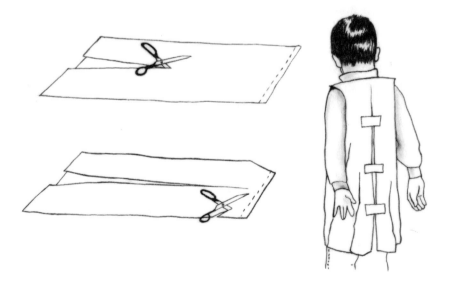

CLOTH PARTY BAGS
• • • • • • • • • • • • • • • • • • • •

THE PRIZE: Party bags are nice to have because they help the guests keep all their game prizes together. The great thing about homemade party bags is that they can be made in any size.

AGE LEVEL: Any age

APPROXIMATE PREPARATION TIME: 15 minutes per bag (not counting drying time of paint)

MATERIALS NEEDED:
- pinking shears
- 5½" × 8" (14 × 20 cm) material—2 pieces per party bag
- fabric paints—various colors (available at crafts stores and superstores)
- 12" (30 cm) shoestrings—1 per party bag
- hot glue gun and glue sticks

PROCEDURE: For each party bag: Using the craft paints, begin by decorating the front side of one piece of material. Be sure to leave about an inch at the top free of decorations. This will be folded over later. The bag will be taller than it is wide, so lay out your material appropriately when decorating it. You can write the guest's name on it, draw zigzag and wavy lines, make dots or other small shapes, whatever you like.

After the paint is dry, use the pinking shears on all four edges of both pieces of material. This will help keep the edges from fraying. Next, fold down towards the back (inside) of the material the top three-quarters of an inch (2 cm) of both the front and back pieces. Hot glue these edges down, being sure to put the hot glue only along the very edge, so that you leave room for a shoestring to be threaded through later.

After the glue has dried, hot glue the front piece to the back piece along the edges, keeping the top folds to the inside and making sure not to glue the top ¾". When this glue is dry, thread the shoestring through both the front and back top edge and tie the ends together. Now the party bags are complete.

HELPFUL HINTS:
- When choosing material for the party bags, try to find some that does not fray too easily.

- Solid colors work better than printed material, unless you don't want to decorate the bags.
- The dimensions given here are just the suggested size and can be changed, if you wish. Just keep in mind that the larger the bag you make, the longer the shoestring needs to be. The shoestring should be at least twice as long as the bag is wide, plus another inch.

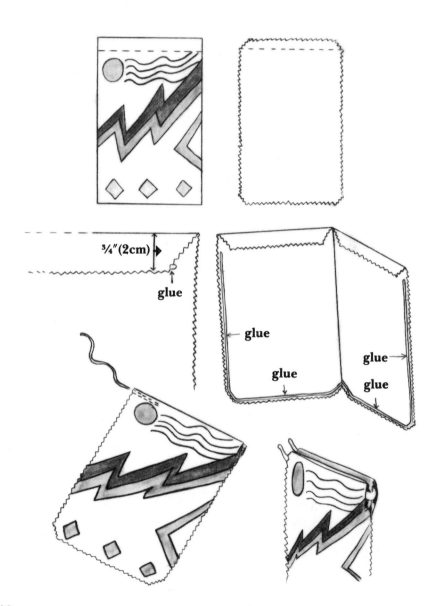

DECORATED CUPS

THE PRIZE: These prizes are really nice because the kids can use them throughout the party and then take them home when the party is over.

AGE LEVEL: Any age

APPROXIMATE PREPARATION TIME: 3–5 minutes per cup

MATERIALS NEEDED:
- plastic cups, any style—1 per prize
- small or medium-sized stickers—3–5 per cup
- paint pens—several colors

PROCEDURE: These cups are very simple to make. Just use your imagination and decorate the cups using the stickers and paint pens in any way you like. Be sure to put each guest's name on the cups so there is no confusion about whose cup is whose.

HELPFUL HINTS:
- Small plastic cups with handles work best for younger children.
- Cups that are wide at the bottom tend not to tip over as easily as cups with narrow bottoms.

GOODY BAGS
• • • • • • • • • • • • •

THE PRIZE: Goody bags are a nice prize to give either at the beginning of a party (so that the kids can munch on the things inside the bags throughout the party) or at the end of a party (so that the kids have some goodies to take home with them).

AGE LEVEL: Any age

APPROXIMATE PREPARATION TIME: 3–5 minutes per bag

MATERIALS NEEDED:
- zipper sandwich bags—1 per prize
- stickers—about 5 per bag
- permanent markers
- several different types of goodies (see suggestions below)

SUGGESTIONS FOR GOODIES: popcorn; pretzels; peanuts; animal crackers; dry cereal; sugarfree chewing gum; cookies; candy; etc. (keeping in mind the age of the guests)

PROCEDURE: Begin by writing each guest's name on a sandwich bag with a permanent marker. Next decorate the bags with the stickers. Then add the goodies and zip the bags closed. If you wish to wrap the goody bags, leave a blank area for the names when decorating them. Then, as the children unwrap them, take a moment to write in the names.

HELPFUL HINT:
- Make sure the goodies that you choose for the bags are appropriate to the ages of the children. For example, do not give two-year-olds such snacks as peanuts or hard candy or other things they can easily choke on.

CANDY CRITTERS

●●●●●●●●●●●●●●●●●●●

THE PRIZE: "Candy critters" are cute little critters with candy-stuffed heads.

AGE LEVEL: Any age

APPROXIMATE PREPARATION TIME: 5 minutes per critter

MATERIALS NEEDED:
- miscellaneous small candies—about 1 handful per critter
- plastic sandwich bags (not ziptop bags)—1 per critter
- 10" (25 cm) squares of plain-colored material
- small rubber bands—1 per critter
- 8" (20 cm) length of curling ribbon—1 per critter
- plastic wiggle eyes (available at crafts stores)—2 per critter
- permanent markers—various colors
- hot glue gun or craft glue

PROCEDURE: Mix all the candies together in a bowl, leaving the wrappers on the individually wrapped ones. *For each candy critter:* Place a handful of the mixed candy in a sandwich bag and place the bag in the center of the square of material. Pull the material up around the bag of candy, securing it with a rubber band. Turn the critter over and spread out the material below the rubber band to help the critter stand. Using a hot glue gun or craft glue, place the eyes on the "head" of the critter. Add a mouth and, if you wish, some hair with the permanent markers. Tie the ribbon around the rubber band to hide it. The candy critters are now finished.

HELPFUL HINTS:
- Some suggestions for small candies include M&Ms, mini marshmallows, gumdrops, gummy candies, and even cereal.
- Remember to keep the ages of the children receiving the candy critters in mind when purchasing the candy. Two- and three-year-olds choke rather easily on hard candy.
- Yarn can also be used to make hair on a candy critter. Use hot glue to stick it on the critter's head.

CANDY CONES

* * * * * * * * * * * * * * * * * *

THE PRIZE: Candy cones are a fun prize, and kids especially enjoy the variety of candy found in them.

AGE LEVEL: Any age

APPROXIMATE PREPARATION TIME: 5–8 minutes per cone

MATERIALS NEEDED:
- flat-bottomed ice cream cones
- plastic wrap, regular or colored
- curling ribbon, 1 or more colors—14" (35 cm) minimum per cone
- candy, small pieces, any variety—about ½ cup per guest

PROCEDURE: Begin by cutting the plastic wrap into pieces approximately 10" × 11½" (25 × 30 cm) and 14" × 11½" (35 cm × 30 cm), one of each size per cone. The measurements do not need to be exact, and all the pieces do not have to be exactly the same size. Next, open the various candies (unless they are individually wrapped) and mix them all together in a bowl. Cut the curling ribbon into 6" (15 cm) and 8" (20 cm) lengths, at least one of each per cone. It's nice to use more than one color of the 8" ribbon per cone.

For each cone: Take one piece of the smaller plastic wrap and place a good-sized handful of the mixed candy in the middle. Pull the edges of the wrap tightly around the candy and tie them with a piece of the shorter curling ribbon. Place the wrapped candy, ribbon and edges side down, inside the cone so that it sort of resembles a scoop of ice cream in the cone. Place the cone in the middle of the larger piece of plastic wrap. Pull the edges up over the cone and the wrapped candy. Tie the wrap in place using at least one piece of the longer strips of ribbon. Curl the edges of the ribbon using the blade of a pair of scissors or some other straight edge, and the candy cone is complete.

HELPFUL HINTS:
- Small children, especially two- and three-year-olds, choke rather easily on small, hard candies. Keep this in mind when selecting the candy for the cones.

- Some good candies to get: M&Ms, colored miniature marsh-mallows, gumdrops, jellybeans, Smarties, etc.

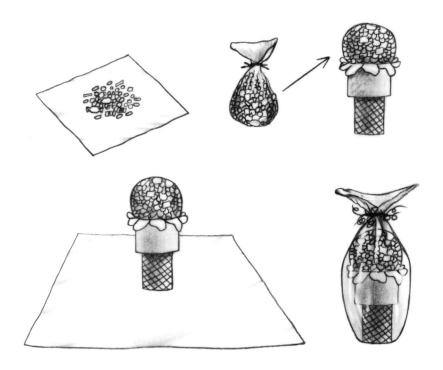

RIBBON WAVERS

THE PRIZE: Ribbon wavers provide a perfect way for children to express themselves while listening to music.

AGE LEVEL: Any age

APPROXIMATE PREPARATION TIME: 5–10 minutes per ribbon waver

MATERIALS NEEDED:
- 2″ (5 cm) wide satin ribbon—3–14 feet (1 m × 4.2 m) per prize, depending on the age of the child
- unsharpened pencils—1 per prize
- 18″ (45 cm) lengths of yarn—1 per prize
- ½″ (13 mm) metal screw-in eyes (available at hardware stores)—1 per prize
- hot glue gun

PROCEDURE: First, screw one metal eye into the eraser end of each pencil. Then, while the hot glue gun is warming up, cut your lengths of ribbon according to this chart:

Age of Child	Length of Ribbon
2 years	3 feet (1 m)
3 years	4 feet (1.2 m)
4 years	6 feet (1.8 m)
5–9 years	10 feet (3 m)
10 and older	14 feet (4.2 m)

When you have finished cutting your ribbon, hot glue ⅛″ (3 mm) hems on each end to help keep them from unravelling. Then, fold and hot glue another half inch of ribbon on one end, being careful not to glue more than the very edge of the ribbon. Also place a dot of hot glue on each metal eye so that the yarn, when placed through the eye, cannot slide off.

When the glue has dried sufficiently, tie one end of each piece of yarn to each eye. Next, thread the other end of the yarn through the half-inch hem on the ribbon. An easy way to do this is to push the pencil through the hem and pull it out the other side until only the yarn is left within the hem. Tie the other end of the yarn about half an inch above the ribbon, forming a triangle through the hem. Now you have a ribbon waver. To use it, just hold the pencil in your hand and swing your arm in wide arcs and circles.

HELPFUL HINTS:

- If you cannot find satin ribbon, other types will also work well. Just keep in mind that lightweight ribbon works better than heavy or stiff ribbon.
- If you do not have a hot glue gun, you can use regular craft glue. Make sure the glue dries completely between the different steps. The material can also be sewn instead of glued.

FEELY BOXES

• • • • • • • • • • • • • •

THE PRIZE: For young children, learning about the shape, size, and texture of objects is fun and easy with a "feely box," making this a great prize for youngsters two to four years old. Older children also enjoy getting this prize because they like trying to trick their friends by placing hard-to-guess items in the box.

AGE LEVEL: Any age

APPROXIMATE PREPARATION TIME: 15–20 minutes per feely box

MATERIALS NEEDED:
- 2-litre soda bottles with a plastic sleeve covering the bottom portion—1 per feely box
- old adult-size socks—1 per feely box (it is okay to use socks that have holes in the heels or toes)
- 4" × 15" (10 × 38 cm) strips of solid-colored contact paper—1 per feely box
- sharp-pointed knife
- scissors
- masking tape

PROCEDURE: For each feely box: Begin by completely cleaning the soda bottle and removing as much of its label as possible. The label need not come off completely. After the bottle is clean, cut off and discard the top portion about 3 inches (7.5 cm) above the plastic sleeve at the bottom. An easy way to do this is to very carefully poke a starting hole with the pointed knife and then cut the rest with scissors. Place masking tape completely around the cut edge of the bottom section, making sure the tape folds over the top of the edge. This will help dull the edge and keep small hands from getting scratched or cut on it.

Next, cut off the socks at the ankle area and discard the foot portion. Slide the sock top down around the taped edge of the soda bottle, covering about 1½ inches (3.75 cm) of the bottle. Tape the sock in place using contact paper, making sure to cover at least the top half-inch of the plastic sleeve so that you cannot see into the bottle without looking through the opening at the top of the sock. The feely box is now complete.

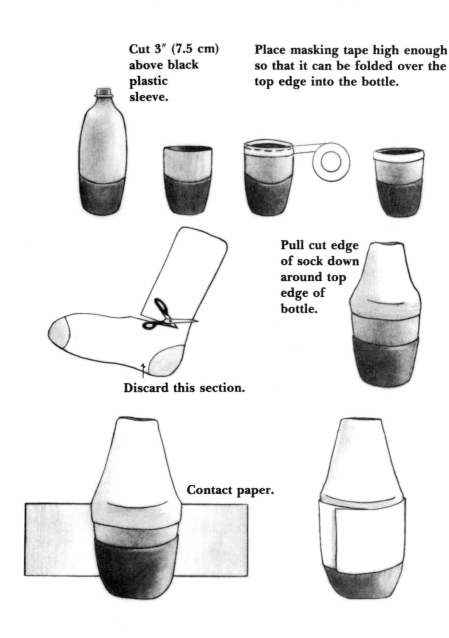

Cut 3″ (7.5 cm) above black plastic sleeve.

Place masking tape high enough so that it can be folded over the top edge into the bottle.

Discard this section.

Pull cut edge of sock down around top edge of bottle.

Contact paper.

To use it, have the child put an object inside while no one is watching (or where no one can see). The child's friends then have to reach into the feely box and, using only their hand, try to guess what the object is.

HELPFUL HINT:

- Long, stretchy socks or cotton socks work better for the feely box than short socks or nylon or polyester socks.

MYSTERY BOTTLES

THE PRIZE: Mystery bottles make interesting prizes. Kids can rock, shake, spin, and roll them around to create myriad unique actions as the two fluids within the bottle try to mix. Then they can watch the two fluids mysteriously separate again.

AGE LEVEL: 3–8

APPROXIMATE PREPARATION TIME: 3–5 minutes per bottle

MATERIALS NEEDED:
- 16-oz. (450 ml) plastic soda bottles with lids—1 per prize
- 1 cup of vinegar per prize
- 1 cup of cooking oil per prize
- food coloring, any color—6 drops per prize
- confetti and/or glitter
- waterproof glue

PROCEDURE: Completely clean the plastic soda bottles and remove as much of the label as possible. Pour 1 cup of vinegar into each bottle. Add the food coloring and mix well. Next, add 1 cup of oil to each bottle and then a handful of confetti and/or glitter. Glue the lids on using the waterproof glue. When the glue is completely dry, the bottles are ready to go.

To enjoy them, simply have the kids rock them back and forth, roll them across the floor, shake them up, and/or spin them around and watch the reactions take place between the oil and the vinegar in the bottle.

HELPFUL HINTS:
- When choosing the oil for this prize, keep in mind that pure corn oil or pure vegetable oil works best. Lighter oils, such as canola or safflower, or even oil blends, tend to break down into much tinier particles when the mystery bottles are shaken, and these particles take longer to re-form.
- 16-oz. bottles are just the suggested size. Other sizes work, too, as long as you stick to the 50/50 proportions for the oil and vinegar.
- If you cannot find waterproof glue, duct tape can be used on the lid to keep it from being removed easily.

HOMEMADE BUBBLES

THE PRIZE: Children always enjoy bubbles, and with this recipe you can make enough for even the largest crowd.

AGE LEVEL: 3–10

APPROXIMATE PREPARATION TIME: 10 minutes

MATERIALS NEEDED:
- liquid dishwashing soap—½ cup
- water—just under 2 cups
- sugar—3 teaspoons
- small unbreakable bottles with screw-on lids—1 per child (old 4-oz. [120 ml] plastic baby bottles work well; use the lids from jars of baby juice for their lids)
- pipe cleaners—1 per child

PROCEDURE: Mix together the dish soap, the water, and the sugar. Pour the solution into the unbreakable bottles. Next, use the pipe cleaners to make a bubble wand for each bottle. To do this, form a circle with one end of the pipe cleaner, twisting the end around the middle of the pipe cleaner. Make sure the resulting bubble wands will fit entirely inside your bottles. Also, ensure that the wands are long enough to easily reach through the tops of the bottles.

HELPFUL HINT:
- Old plastic baby bottles can be found at many yard sales. Be sure not to use glass jars for the bubble solution, because bubbles tend to splash out when removing the wand from the bottles and spill onto the outside of the bottles, causing them to become rather slippery.

BUBBLE MACHINE

THE PRIZE: Kids love bubbles, and these simple bubble machines add a new dimension to bubble blowing.

AGE LEVEL: 4 and older (younger children might drink the bubble solution)

APPROXIMATE PREPARATION TIME: 5 minutes per bubble machine

MATERIALS NEEDED:
- small margarine tubs with lids—1 per bubble machine
- flexible drinking straws—1 per bubble machine
- stickers
- hole punch
- paint pens—various colors
- mini bottles of bubble solution—1 per bubble machine

PROCEDURE: Thoroughly clean the margarine tubs and lids. Using the hole punch, make two holes on each lid. Each hole should be near the edge on opposite sides of the lid. Decorate the margarine tubs with the stickers and paint pens. Place the lids on the tubs. Next, take the flexible straws and cut them in half, discarding the end without the flex section. Place a straw in one hole in each of the margarine tubs. The bubble machines are now finished. Next, write each prospective party guest's name on a sticker and set the stickers aside. When the children receive this prize, quickly add the sticker with each child's name to their bubble machine.

To use, simply remove the lids and pour about two inches (5 cm) of bubble solution inside. Replace the lid and blow through the straw. The bubbles will tumble out the other hole in a long chain. Remind the children not to drink the bubbles.

HELPFUL HINTS:
- The bottles of bubble solution can be given as a separate prize.
- Homemade bubbles can also be used (see recipe on page 110).

INSECT HOMES
• • • • • • • • • • • • • • • •

THE PRIZE: All kids love to catch bugs, and these insect homes make a perfect "motel" for their little guests when they catch them.

AGE LEVEL: 3–12

APPROXIMATE PREPARATION TIME: 5 minutes per insect home

MATERIALS NEEDED:
- 2-litre soda bottles with lids—one per insect home
- old nylons or knee-highs—one leg per insect home
- sharp-pointed knife
- scissors

PROCEDURE: Begin by cleaning the soda bottles and then removing as much of the labels from them as possible. Soaking the bottles in warm water for 20–30 minutes may help. Rinse them thoroughly.

After removing the labels, follow these directions for each insect home: Cut out a panel about 5″ × 6″ (12.5 × 15 cm) from the center area of one side of the soda bottle. The easiest way to cut the panel is to take a sharp-pointed knife and very carefully poke a starting hole in the center of the area you will be cutting. Then use scissors to cut the panel out. This "window" allows the insects to breathe. Place the lid on the bottle. Take the nylons and cut off one leg about 4 inches (10 cm) below the crotch area, or use a knee-high. Place the soda bottle in the leg, making sure to push the bottle all the way to the bottom. The part of the stocking above the bottle is used as a carrying handle. To use the insect home, have the child catch a bug, remove the lid from the soda bottle, put the bug in, and replace the lid.

HELPFUL HINTS:
- Be sure to explain to the children that bugs should not be kept in the insect homes for more than a few hours.
- Having the children add some fresh grass, leaves and twigs might make them more conscious of the insect's needs as well as making the insect's stay in its temporary home a little more pleasant.

Cut out
this section.

HOMEMADE PLAYDOUGH

THE PRIZE: Playdough is something that all kids love because it's easy to manipulate. This recipe is quick and simple to make.

AGE LEVEL: 3–12

APPROXIMATE PREPARATION TIME: 10 minutes per batch or double batch

MATERIALS NEEDED:
- 1 cup each flour and water
- ½ cup salt
- 1 tablespoon cooking oil
- 2 teaspoons cream of tartar
- food coloring—8–10 drops per batch
- storage containers—(zip-top sandwich bags or small margarine tubs with lids work well)—1 per prize

PROCEDURE: One batch is enough for 4 prizes. Mix all the ingredients together in a medium-sized or large saucepan. Cook over medium heat, stirring constantly. Within a few minutes, the mixture will begin to ball up and change consistency. When the mixture, which will now be a ball, no longer feels sticky to the touch, place it on a sheet of waxed paper or on a Formica-topped surface and knead immediately. After the substance has cooled completely, separate it into balls and place them in sandwich bags or small margarine tubs, 1 per guest. This mixture does not have to be refrigerated, and, if properly taken care of, will last for weeks.

HELPFUL HINT:
- It is best with this recipe not to make more than a double batch at one time.

BUTTON SPINNERS

THE PRIZE: Button spinners are very easy prizes to make, and they can keep a child occupied for quite a while.

AGE LEVEL: 5–12

APPROXIMATE PREPARATION TIME: 3–5 minutes per spinner

MATERIALS NEEDED:
- 40″ (100 cm) lengths of yarn—1 per spinner
- large, flat button with at least 2 holes—1 per spinner

PROCEDURE: Take a length of yarn and thread it through the two holes on the button. If the button has four holes, thread the yarn through the two holes that are diagonal from each other. Tie the ends of the yarn together. This will form a big loop with the button on it. The button spinner is now ready.

To use it, spread out the loop of yarn so that the button passes through both strands of the loop. Hook each end of the loop over the pointer finger of each hand. Center the button. Now swing the button around in circles between your hands to wind it up. Five to eight swings is usually enough. When the button is wound up, gently pull your hands apart and let the action of the button pull your hands back towards each other. Continue gently pulling your hands apart and then letting the button pull your hands back towards each other for as long as you wish. With practice, the button will "sing" as it spins.

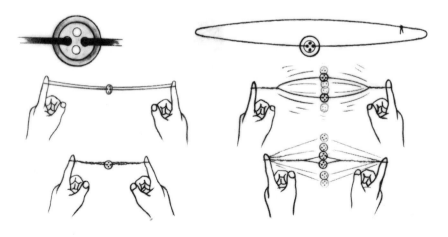

HELPFUL HINTS:

- The size of the button is very important. The smaller the button, the harder it is to get the action going. Generally, the button should be a least the size of a quarter (24 mm in diameter), preferably larger.
- You may want to practice using the button spinner so that you can show the kids how it works.

PRIZE SUGGESTIONS
• •

Most of these prizes are pretty common and you can purchase them at party supply stores by the dozen for a reasonable price. One-dollar stores are also a great source for prizes as well as other party supplies, and catalogues specializing in party supplies are yet a third source of neat prizes at good prices.

Ages 2 and Older:

Small posters
Lollipops
Large whistles
Necklaces
Stuffed animals
Novelty T-shirts
Sunglasses
Board books
Large superballs
Mini boxes of cereal
Children's place mats
Coloring books

Fingerpaints
Bracelets
Miniature candy bars—no nuts
Kazoos
Hats—all varieties
Pails and shovels
Beach balls
Bouncing balls—all sizes
Small boxes of animal crackers
Helium balloons
Puzzles with 3–6 pieces
Trading cards

Toy figures—such as army figures
Stickers—all sizes, regular and scented
Pre-blown balloons—regular and shaped
Plastic animals, such as dinosaurs or zoo animals
Beanbags (these should be well sewn so that no small beans slip out)
Novelty toothbrushes (for younger children, find toothbrushes with short handles)

Ages 3 and Older:

Small flashlights
Puzzles with 6–12 pieces
Posable/bendable figures
Rings
Fun buttons
Go Fish cards
Ponytail holders
Combs—shaped or designed
Chalk
Pencils—regular and colored
Erasers—regular and shaped
Playdough
Scissors
Silly straws
Bubbles
Storybooks
Prism viewers

Novelty key chains
Hand-held bead puzzles
Toy cars
Temporary tattoos
Old Maid cards
Frisbees
Barrettes
Coin purses
Pens—all colors of ink
Pencil toppers
Water paints
Stampers and stamp pads
Construction paper
Pencil boxes
Play harmonicas
Finger puppets
Mini magic screens

Notepads—especially novelty ones
Crayons—fat, regular, scented, glitter, etc.
Bubble wands—these usually hook onto pencils
Headbands—plain or with wobble toppers
Markers—regular, fat tip, skinny tip, double tip, scented, etc.
Preschool flash cards, featuring colors, shapes, numbers, and
    letters

Ages 4 and Older:

Water balloons
Slide puzzles
Magnifying glass
Face masks
Squirt guns
Superballs—any size
Playing cards
Stencils
Pompom critters
Balsa-wood gliders
Sparkling spinners
Vinyl spring pop-ups
Wax lips
Novelty candles
Puzzles with 12–63 pieces
   (oversized)
Clackers—hand-held and finger
Glue—regular, colored, sticks, etc.
Rubber noses, fingers, and other gag gifts
Penny banks (with a nickel or two to start them off)

Kites
Silly putty
Paper dolls
Glide balls
Vinyl water squirters
Glitter glue pens
Paper yo-yos
Balloon whistles
Whirling whistle tubes
Mini surprise cans
Mini spin tops

Ages 5 and Older:

Novelty magnets
Regular yo-yos
Rulers
Stationery
Flash cards with words
Paddle balls

Activity books
Pocket portfolios
Spiral notebooks
Jacks
Drop poppers
Easy reader books

Ages 6 and Older:

Joke books
Beginner novels
Champagne party poppers
Puzzles with 50 or more pieces
Flash cards with numbers (addition and subtraction)

Comic books
Bookmarks
Paper doorknob hangers

THINGS TO SAVE
THROUGHOUT THE YEAR
• •

The following list contains common everyday items that are needed for many of the games, activities, and homemade prizes in this book. The easiest way to keep track of the items you save is to place them all in the same place, such as a large box kept in a closet or garage. Then, when the time comes to play a game, do an activity, or make some prizes, you will be able to save time and maybe even money, because you will already have collected some of the needed materials.

1) pieces of yarn and string
2) index cards
3) old magazines
4) shoe boxes
5) paper clips
6) popsicle sticks—all sizes
7) plastic straws
8) buttons—all sizes
9) old socks
10) old nylons and knee-highs
11) plastic grocery bags
12) old catalogs and store ads
13) clothespins (both spring type and plain)
14) rubber bands
15) fabric scraps
16) old newspapers
17) old T-shirts
18) tissue paper—all colors
19) pieces of contact paper
20) curling ribbon
21) baby food jars—these can be used to keep smaller items you are saving sorted
22) plastic soda bottles—all sizes (especially 16 oz. and 2-litre bottles)
23) plastic fruit containers (such as strawberries come in)
24) cardboard boxes of all sizes (flatten these for storage)
25) new pencils (not sharpened) with erasers
26) small magnets (especially strong ones)
27) wrapping paper (scraps as well as larger pieces)
28) small plastic butter bowls with lids
29) old bottles of white or light-colored fingernail polish
30) plastic toys that float without turning over
31) old pieces of lumber, especially 2″ × 4″ scraps (about 6″ or 15 cm long)
32) lightweight cardboard pieces (such as those found at the back of notepads)—all sizes

33) medicine dosage cups (be sure to clean them really well)
34) lids to baby juice jars (to use with plastic baby bottles when making bubbles)
35) strips of tracking holes from continuous-form computer paper

LOOK FOR THE FOLLOWING ITEMS AT YARD SALES:
1) 4-oz. (120 ml) *plastic* baby bottles
2) plastic or metal bangle bracelets (for ring toss)
3) plastic gems—all sizes, shapes, and colors
4) colorful beads—I get a lot of these by buying necklaces at yard sales and then cutting them apart

PATTERNS

(All patterns in this section may be copied for use with this book.)

FISH PATTERN
• • • • • • • • • • • • • • • • •
GAME: "Fishing for Treasure"

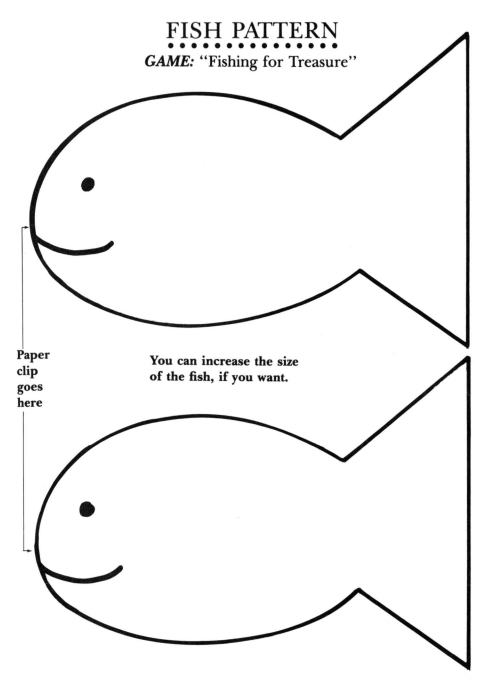

**Paper
clip
goes
here**

**You can increase the size
of the fish, if you want.**

CRAZY CRITTER PATTERN #1

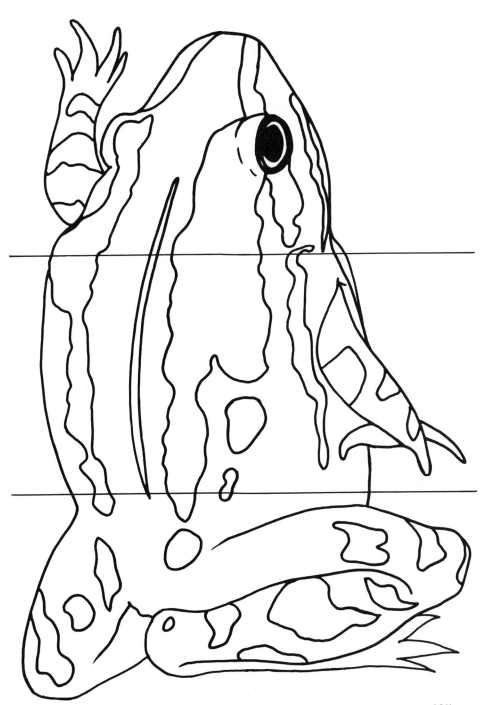

126

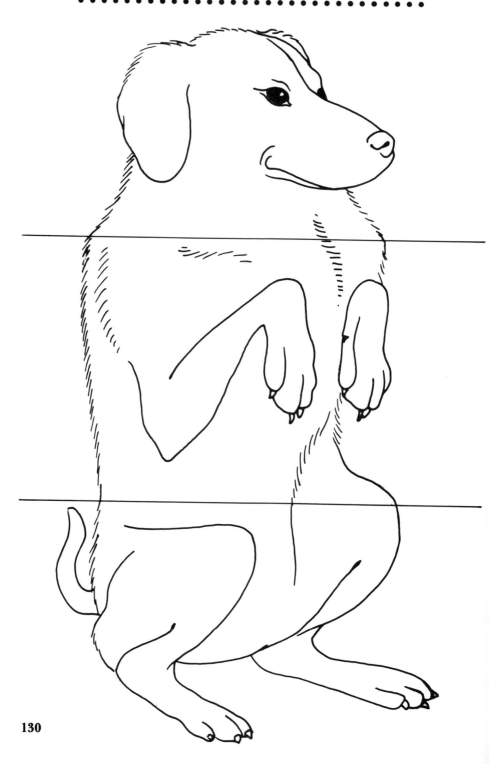

131

132

SAMPLE CARDS TO COPY
FOR "BALLOON BELLIES"

bandage	screw	cotton swab	key
paper clip	marble or superball	short pencil	die
puzzle piece	whistle	safety pin	toy car
button	ring	necklace	jingle bell

CLOWN FOOT
• • • • • • • • • • • • • • •

ACTIVITY: "Clown Wigs and Feet"

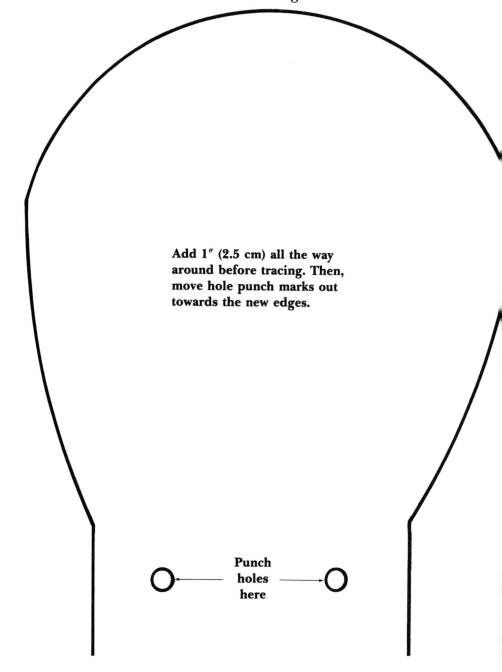

Add 1″ (2.5 cm) all the way
around before tracing. Then,
move hole punch marks out
towards the new edges.

Punch
holes
here

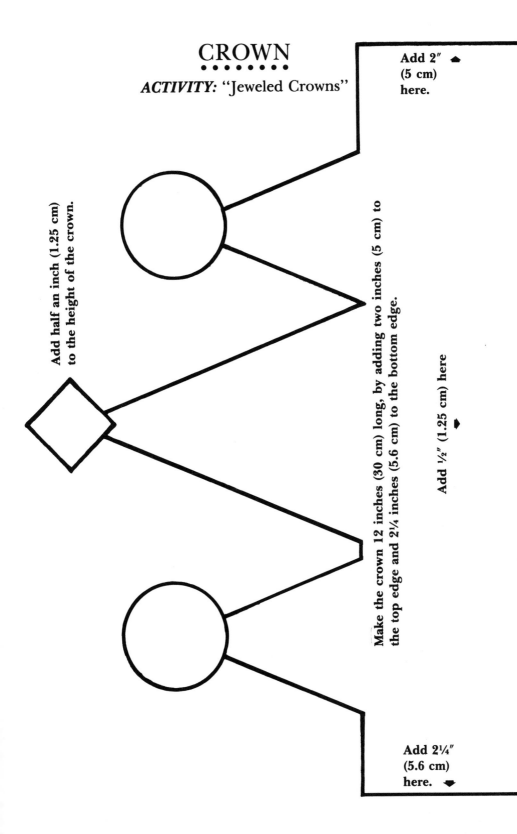

CROWN
• • • • • • • • •
ACTIVITY: "Jeweled Crowns"

Add 2″ (5 cm) here.

Add half an inch (1.25 cm) to the height of the crown.

Make the crown 12 inches (30 cm) long, by adding two inches (5 cm) to the top edge and 2¼ inches (5.6 cm) to the bottom edge.

Add ½″ (1.25 cm) here

Add 2¼″ (5.6 cm) here.

GUEST LIST

	Name	Age	Phone Number	Yes	No
1					
2					
3					
4					
5					
6					
7					
8					
9					
10					
11					
12					
13					
14					
15					

Special instructions for parents when they RSVP _____

_____

SPECIAL FEATURES CHART
AND INDEX

Key: A   Collaborative or helping   E   Stimulates creativity and
           behavior   imagination
       B   Sharing   F   Team effort
       C   Communication and   G   Skill building (physical)
           listening skills   H   For children with
       D   Stimulates thinking and   learning differences or
           reasoning   physical challenges

Game/Activity	Page	Age	Key	Players	Setup	Length	Belief
Ancient Treasure Dig	35	3–10	E/G	1–6+	10+	20	
Animal Antics	58	6–12	C/E	2–16	10	10	I am capable. I am creative.
Baby Huey	29	3–8	H	2 up	5	10	
Balloon Bellies	41	4–8	A/G	1–15	15	15	I am capable.
Balloon Hunt	17	1–3		4 up	15	10	I am capable.
Bell Catcher	81	3–10	B/E/G/H	1–8	10	10	I am capable.
Bob-a-Doughnut	25	2–10		1–8+	15	10	I am capable.
Bubble Blowing Fun	67	3–8	E/H	1–12	10	15	I am creative.
Bubble Mania	30	4–8	H	1 up	10	10	I am capable.
Chalk Up a Prize	43	4–8	D/G	3–8	15	10	I am capable.
Clown Wigs and Feet	68	3–8	B/E/G/H	1–8	20	15	I am capable. I am creative.

Game/Activity	Page	Age	Key	Players	Setup	Length	Belief
Cookie Decorating	88	3–12	B/E/G/H	1–8	10	15	I am capable. I am creative. I have something to contribute.
Crazy Critters	33	3–10	E	3–15	10	15	I am capable. I am creative.
Dinosaur Bones	22	2–8	E/G	1–8	10	30+	I am capable. I am creative.
Dr. Knots	53	5–12	A/D/E/F	5–20	0	10+	I am capable. I belong.
Face Painting Fun	95	7–12	A/E/G/H	1–8	5+	15	I am capable. I am creative. I have something to contribute.
Fishing for Treasure	18	2–8	F/G/H	1–12+	20	6+	I am capable. I can learn a skill.
Foamy Fun	57	6–12	C	2–12	5	20	I am capable.
Gold Digger	24	2–10	A/H	1–8+	10	5	I am capable.
Incredible Shrinking Prize	20	2–8	B/H	3–8+	30	10	I am capable.

Key: A Collaborative or helping behavior
      B Sharing
      C Communication and listening skills
      D Stimulates thinking and reasoning
      E Stimulates creativity and imagination
      F Team effort
      G Skill building (physical)
      H For children with learning differences or physical challenges

Game/Activity	Page	Age	Key	Players	Setup	Length	Belief
Jeweled Crowns	77	3–8	B/E/G/H	1–8	15+	15	I am capable. I am creative.
Midnight Prizes	32	3–8		1–12	10	5	I am capable. I can be adventurous.
Mystical Magical Dough	84	3–12	C/E/H	1 up	5	15	I am creative.
Notable Necklaces	90	5–12	B/E/G/H	1–8	15	10	I am capable. I am creative.
Paint a Hat or Visor	92	5–12	B/E/G/H	1–8	5+	15	I am capable. I am creative.
Paint a Shirt	96	6–12	B/E/G/H	1–8	5+	15	I am capable. I am creative.
Paper Bag Puppets	79	3–10	B/E/G/H	1–8	10	15	I am capable. I am creative.
Paper Cup Phones	71	3–8	B/E/G/H	1–8	10	10	I am capable.
Paper Plate Masks	74	3–8	B/E/G/H	1–8	15+	20	I am capable. I am creative.
Penny Pots	37	3–12	E/G	1–16	15	15	
Playdough Fun	64	2–8	E/G/H	1 up	5+	15	I am creative.
Pop-a-Loony	27	3–8	G	3–12	20	15	I can do silly things. I can have a good time.
Pop-a-Prize #1	51	5–11	G	1–10	25	10	I am capable.

Game/Activity	Page	Age	Key	Players	Setup	Length	Belief
Pop-a-Prize #2	51	3–5	G	1–10	20	20	I am capable.
Puzzling Puzzles	49	4–12	A/C/E/F/G	1 up	5+	10+	I am capable. I have value. I have worth. I belong. I have some-thing to contribute. I am resource-ful. I count.
Riddle Hunt	55	6–12	A/D/E	1–16	20+	15	I am capable. I have value. I have worth. I have some-thing to contribute. I am resource-ful. I count.
Ring Around the Reindeer	39	3–12	G/H	1–10	20	10	It's okay not to not make it the first time.
Scavenger Hunt	45	4–8	C/D	1–8	35	15	I am capable. I am resource-ful.

Key:
A Collaborative or helping behavior
B Sharing
C Communication and listening skills
D Stimulates thinking and reasoning
E Stimulates creativity and imagination
F Team effort
G Skill building (physical)
H For children with learning differences or physical challenges

Game/Activity	Page	Age	Key	Players	Setup	Length	Belief
Scrumptious Flowers	82	3–10	B/E/G/H	1–8	5	10	I am capable. I am creative.
Shaving Cream Fun	62	2–8	E/G/H	1 up	5	20	I am creative. It's okay to be messy and have fun.
Sprinkler Fun	65	2–10	C	1–6+	5	20	
Tambourines	72	3–8	B/E/G/H	1–6	10	10	I am capable. I am creative.
Toy Afloat	15	1–3	G/H	4–5+	5	5	I am capable.
Treasure Boxes	86	3–12	B/E/G/H	1–8	15+	15	I am capable. I am creative.
Treasure Hunt	47	4–10	A/D/F	2–12	30	15	I am capable. I have value. I have worth. I belong. I have something to contribute. I am resourceful. I count.
Wonderful Water Play	61	2–6	G/H	1–9	5+	20	

Author **Jody Blosser** has been working with young children for over 20 years, first in day care centers, and for the last nine years, running her own home day care. She wrote this book because she feels it is important for young children to have games and activities they can play together as a group without feeling threatened or incompetent because they keep losing. She lives in St. Peters, Missouri, with her husband, three young children, and two tankfuls of guppies.

Gaylyn Larned, LCSW, Ph.D, has been practicing psychotherapy for almost 25 years, specializing in work with children and adults with Attention Deficit Disorder, and other learning differences, as well as relationship dependency and obsessive-compulsive disorders. She is co-founder with her husband, psychotherapist Edward Hicks, of Turning Point Center for Self-Realization and Active-Self-Empowerment. Together they also created LearningWorks for Kids and co-founded The Learning House, which offers cutting-edge programs that teach children as well as adults how to use their brains and minds more effectively and creatively. She lives in Westport, Connecticut, with her husband, her Bijon, Maggie, and her husband's lilac-pointed Himalayan cat, Maya.

INDEX